Social Accounting Systems

SOCIAL ACCOUNTING
SYSTEMS

by

M. YANOVSKY

ALDINE PUBLISHING COMPANY

CHICAGO

Preface

Social accounting grew up as a result of the desire to bring together in a meaningful and comprehensive manner all the available observed facts on the economic and financial activity of a nation.

Three social accounting systems of flow have been developed during the last three decades. Each of these systems has been constructed separately and independently. The framework of each system is constructed to tackle specific aspects of the national economy. It is also designed in a manner which helps in framing policies for future activity.

The aim of this book is mainly to describe the anatomy of these three social accounting systems and compare their structures. Some attention is also given to a comparison of the systems in actual use by some industrially developed countries, including the USSR. The problem of integrating the three systems is also cursorily treated.

Most of the material in this book was originally submitted as a doctor's thesis in the University of Manchester. A number of critical observations and arguments have been omitted here, and some descriptive material added.

Various statistical offices and other institutions have kindly provided me with unpublished data and information for which I am greatly indebted. I wish, in particular, to thank the Statistical office of the United Nations in New York; the Statistics Section of the European Office of the United Nations in Geneva, and the flow of funds and savings section of the Federal Reserve System in Washington.

To Mr John P. Lewis I am indebted for all the observations he made when I first outlined the scheme of my study in a graduate seminar at the University of Manchester.

I also wish to thank Dr R. C. Geary and Mr K. S. Lomax who criticized the study and made various suggestions.

My deepest gratitude goes to Professor Charles F. Carter for his painstaking guidance and constructive criticism.

Any mispresentations or errors committed are to be attributed to me only.

Tel Aviv   M. YANOVSKY

October 1964

Contents

vii

CHAPTER V: INTEGRATION OF THE SOCIAL
ACCOUNTING SYSTEMS

Introduction

I · ACCENT ON MACROECONOMIC STUDY AND ANALYSIS

The two world wars of this century, and the social and political revolutions which followed them, have given great impetus to the study and analysis of macroeconomic problems. Confronted with acute economic and financial difficulties of international scale and character, the people and their respective governments have encouraged economists to examine the economic and financial activities of the different sectors in an economy from the point of view of the nation as a whole.

Two related factors helped greatly in the study and analysis of macroeconomic problems. Firstly, there was a tremendous expansion of enterprises of all sorts in the form of private and public corporations and co-operatives. Not only were many new enterprises established in each country, and particularly in the industrially developed countries, but also many existing corporations and co-operatives combined to form still larger ones. The second factor was the growing force of organized labour. Unions and other organizations of workers were not only interested in fostering macroeconomic enquiries, but were in a position to assist them with reliable data and information.

It should perhaps be added that the prevailing tendency during the last decades in almost all industrially developed countries, to varying degree, has been for more state intervention, control and planning.

It was the growth of large enterprises, the establishment of various

organizations and institutions to serve both the enterprises on one
hand, and the consumers, on the other, and the increasing organizational strength of the labour force, that made extensive, continued,
and reliable statistical work possible.

II · FROM PARTIAL ECONOMIC INDICES AND AGGREGATES TO SYSTEMS OF GENERAL INTERDEPENDENCE

Up to the beginning of the second world war all quantitative economic and financial data, and all the related statistical techniques and
methods which were concurrently developed, took the form either
of indices of price levels, productive activity and employment, or
of trends in financial activity. It was only during the second world
war and immediately after it, that economists and statisticians
realized that these aggregated data could not only help greatly in the
vigorous and disciplined thinking of theoreticians, but (which is
more important) could be of immediate practical use and interest to
government authorities, to large enterprises, to labour organizations
and to all other similar decision-making bodies. Economic statisticians also became convinced that only a system of interlocking
aggregates – an articulated framework – could disclose any inco-
herence in the data collected from different and varied sources. It
could, at the same time, bring into light the areas of ignorance and
the missing links of data and information.

Three methodological systems were soon developed. One system
attempts primarily to measure the national income, final product,
consumption, and accumulation of capital. The second system is
largely devoted to the presentation of the inter-industrial process of
production and the movement of commodities. The main role of the
third system is to show how production processes, consumption,
and investment are currently financed. The common denominator
of these three systems is that they all deal with the 'flowing' process
of economic and financial activities. They describe the flow of the
contributions of labour to production and the reverse flow of income
labour receives from productive enterprises; they show the flow of

intermediate commodities between the various branches of national industry and the flow of finished goods to consumers. Such systems also display the circular financial flows which permit real goods and services to flow between the various large segments of the economy.

Each of the above systems has been independently constructed, mainly during the last three decades, and has been put into extensive practical and theoretical use, particularly in the industrially developed countries of the western world. These methodological sets of accounts became commonly known as social accounting systems – a term originally suggested by Professor Hicks [21, p. 224]. They are, in the chronological order of their development:

(a) The 'national accounts' system.

(b) The 'input-output' system.

(c) The 'flow of funds' system.

It is to the study of these social accounting systems that this book is devoted.

III · THE GENERAL SCOPE AND AIMS OF THE STUDY

Chapter I of the study gives a general description of the underlying concepts, definitions and basic structure of social accounts. Though the description will refer primarily to the National Accounts, a first approach to the analysis of the concepts underlying the other two systems will also be made here. It will also be shown, in a general manner, how the concepts and definitions of the social accounts can and do vary with different types of economy.

In Chapter II there is an analytical comparison of the structural and conceptual similarities and differences of specific national accounts systems. The two 'international' systems, i.e. the national accounts system as proposed by the United Nations [40] and the national accounts system as recommended by the Organization for European Economic Co-operation – OEEC [28] are described and analysed. There follows a description of the national accounts of the United Kingdom and those of the United States. The national accounts systems of these two countries are compared with the

systems designed by the international organizations. The presentation of the system in a matrix form brings out clearly to what extent
the accounts are constructed on a 'from-whom-to-whom' basis.

Since the national accounts serve also as a basic source for income
analysis, it is shown how various identities of flows and aggregates
can be derived from the explicit flows and aggregates in the recommended United Nations accounts system.

Two tables are given which demonstrate how the two major
aggregates of national income and gross national product at market
price can be measured either by income flows or by expenditure
flows in each of the four systems mentioned. Such comparisons give
a bird's-eye-view of the major structural similarities and differences
of these systems.

A national accounts system which deviates in many respects from
those in popular use in most of the western countries is that of
France. The system is also in use in most of the countries which are
or have been under French political, economic, and cultural influence. In the analytical description of this sytem special attention
is paid to the financial flows which are combined here with the other
flows of production, consumption, and capital formation.

Chapter II also contains a description of USSR concepts and
definitions of national income. The description is based primarily
on textbooks on national income written by Russian experts. A
Russian textbook in the field of economics and finance could probably be regarded as a semi-official publication. Some important
basic information has also been derived from an internal study of the
subject carried out by the statistical office of the United Nations,
and the observations of the central statistical board of the USSR on
this study.

Some specific recommendations are made for the integration of
the domestic and national income accounts of the United Nations
system with those of the USSR accounts. It is also shown how the
available published data on the income accounts of the UK and the
USA for 1950 and 1960 could be recalculated according to USSR
concepts.

In the final part of Chapter II the problem of presenting a comprehensive system of national accounts in constant prices is considered. The possibilities and the difficulties involved are indicated, and some recommendations are made as to how this task could be achieved.

Chapter III gives a brief discussion of the input-output system. Though the input-output system is primarily concerned with inter-industrial relationships, it is also interrelated with the final demands and primary inputs as independent exogenous parts of its framework. It expresses the output of the various productive industries as a function of final demands. This is particularly so in the case of the open model of the input-output system. The systematized statistical data on final demands and primary inputs, again, lie mainly within the sphere of the national accounts; hence the rather close connexion between the open model of the input-output system and the national accounts system. The development of the input-output system began, however, with the closed model. The input-output system is first described, therefore, in terms of the closed model, the early version of the system, which is at present no longer in practical use. The open model is then described with the aim of demonstrating in particular the special properties of the open model as a forecasting and planning instrument. It is pointed out how, unlike the national accounts system or the flow of funds system (which show primarily the economic and financial activities of a period in the past), the input-output system can also serve as an explicit indicator for future productive activities, particularly where the whole or part of the productive activity of a nation is centrally planned.

The flow of funds system and other versions of this system are critically treated in Chapter IV. The national transactions accounts of Canada and the expanded accounts of France, which have been influenced by the flow of funds system and are in a sense adapted versions of the system, are also critically described and analysed.

In comparing the parallel features of the American flow of funds system and the other two versions of financial transactions accounts mentioned, some suggestions are offered as to how an economy should be sectorized for financial flows. Some recommendations are also made in connexion with the financial transaction categories of these systems.

While each of the three social accounting systems of flow and their varied versions are treated separately in Chapters II to IV, Chapter V gives an overall comparative analytical description of all the three systems. This inter-system comparison is brought out particularly in connexion with the tendency to integrate all the social accounting systems.

The problem of integrating the social accounting systems, particularly those of the national accounts and the financial transactions accounts, is actually only at the discussion stage among statistical experts.

It is argued that while the national accounts can be integrated with the input-output system, the financial transactions accounts cannot be integrated with these two systems.

CHAPTER ONE

National Accounts Systems – Concepts and Definitions

I · ORIGINS

A. EARLY INQUIRIES INTO NATIONAL INCOME AGGREGATES

The interest of economists in determining the level of national income of a nation and its distribution among the various sectors – productive and non-productive – of the population can be traced to the 17th century. The 'political arithmetician' Gregory King made in 1696 an inquiry into 'The Annual Income, and Expense of the Nation, at it stood Anno 1688' [8] (This inquiry and other 'Natural and Political Observations and Conclusions upon the State and Condition of England 1696 by Gregory King Esq., Lancaster Herald' are subjoined in George Chalmers' 'An Estimate of the Comparative Strength of Great Britain'.) The contribution of this work lies mainly in the fact that information on the 'income flow' of a nation as compared with the 'wealth' of a nation had been provided.

It was, however, only after the First World War that economists began to apply their analytical power and statistical tools to the measurement of current production and the distribution of its fruit.

From scattered statistical data, Professor Bowley compiled and calculated the average wages and aggregate earnings of the working population since 1860, and Sir Josiah Stamp adjusted information on the amount of taxable income as far back as 1847.

More consistent and continuous, though not particularly systematic, statistical work was then also started by Government statistical offices in most western countries. These offices began to compile the necessary information and make appropriate computations of various income, expenditure and product aggregates, inter-related also with demographic statistics. At the same time, economists and statisticians have contributed a great deal to the analysis of these data. With their interest in income analysis they have gradually built up the theoretical background for a national income accounting system. The studies of Sir Josiah Stamp [5] and of Professor Bowley [4] instigated by the National Institute of Economic and Social Research have been a great stimulus for wider and deeper empirical observations on income, consumption, and savings. Professor C. Clark [9] not only computed and analyzed all the major national income aggregates, but also suggested clear definitions of the concepts of national income. In the United States, Professor Kuznets [26] has started a series of thorough studies on national income and its composition which served as a background to national accounts systems as are in use now.

However, the construction of a systematic framework into which the national income, expenditure, and accumulation of capital aggregates could be arranged in a way that the inter-relation between them could be clearly seen and grasped was left to the days of the Second World War and immediately after it.

B. THE IMPACT OF BUSINESS ACCOUNTANCY ON THE NATIONAL ACCOUNTS SYSTEMS

Systematic accounting systems for private trade and business firms are known to have been in existence for at least five centuries. The most popular and widely used of these was that laid down in principle towards the end of the 15th century by Lucas Pacioli, an Italian Franciscan monk, in his 'de computis et scripturis' [14]. Pacioli, who was a close friend of Leonardo da Vinci, was a mathematician, and connected in various ways with the commerical world of those days.

The three most important principles of this private business accounting system, in their impact upon the national accounts system, are as follows.

Firstly, any individual, either in his capacity as a consumer or as a producer, any enterprise, whether owned by one or several individuals, and any organization or institution, can be regarded as a book-keeping unit, or accounting entity. Secondly, there exist two types of transaction: a transaction of flow – actual or imputed – which is either an income or an expense of the book-keeping unit, whose combined flows during a stated period of time comprise the items of an income and expense statement; and a tranasction of change in the status and composition of the assets and liabilities of the book-keeping unit, or an addition or decrease in the status of wealth of the unit. This is why the residual between the income and expense – positive or negative – of a stated period of time, constitutes a transaction of change in the assets or liabilities. The description of the status of the entity's assets and liabilities at a fixed date constitutes its balance sheet. Thirdly, transactions of flow and transactions of change in wealth are inter-related. This interdependence characterizes the whole book-keeping system.

It is because of these basic principles that the business book-keeping system has been successfully used alike by small and by large and multiple firms.

Viewing the various groups of transactors or sections of an economy as subsidiaries of the whole national economy, and the whole economy as the central accounting unit, enabled economic statisticians to adapt the business accounting system as an accounting framework for national economc activity. Such adaptation, they realized, could conveniently be applied to present a systematic measurement of national income, of expenditure on the national product, and of accumulation of national wealth and other economic flow aggregates. It could be used to demonstrate the interrelationships between these flows and aggregates. It could in fact also be adapted for the presentation of statements of wealth or national balance sheets.

C. DEVELOPMENTS SINCE THE SECOND WORLD WAR

The National accounts system began, as already indicated, to take its final shape during the Second World War, and, with increasing momentum, immediately after it. The complicated economic problems which the war produced, encouraged economists in the academic world and in official circles to establish a methodological system for the measurement of national production and the national income it generates. The international organizations established during the forties also sought a comprehensive and uniform statistical tool which could be used for the international comparison of economic activity.

By 1947 the United Kingdom, the United States, Australia, Canada, Ireland, and the Netherlands had formulated and put into use complete and inter-related national accounts systems. These accounts already provided the methodological estimates of national product, national income and its distribution by factors of production, private and public consumption, and capital formation aggregates.

It was in 1947, also, that the sub-committee on national income statistics of the League of Nations Committee of statistical experts issued its report on 'Measurement of National Income and the Construction of Social Accounts'. To this report was attached a memorandum submitted by Richard Stone – who acted as chairman of the above committee – on 'definition and measurement of the national income and related totals' [39]. Though a number of changes have since been introduced in the national accounts system proposed by the international organizations, this memorandum remains nevertheless a basic study in concepts, definitions, and taxonomic problems. The selection and definition of the economic aggregates have been clearly influenced by Keynesian thought – a fact which has been pointed out by Professor Stone. Applying an accounting framework to the Keynesian theory brought out clearly what data and what classification of data are required to establish a meaningful, useful, and convenient method for applying it to policy making.

D. ADVANTAGES AND PRACTICAL USES

There are many reasons for the fact that national accounts have rapidly gained such exceptional popularity among political and social leaders, industrialists and economists. The main advantages of the system and its practical applications could be summarized as follows:

1. The national accounts were drawn up with the view of helping the public authorities in formulating their economic and fiscal policies. This use of the national accounts to exert active public influence on economic development is still of great importance. The abundance of facts organized in an inter-related manner are guides to a study of cause and effect in economic activity. Even in developing countries where some of the statistical estimates in the accounts are liable to be not as precise as is desirable, the accounts as a whole are nevertheless of guiding value to decision-making in public policy.

The use of the national accounts for the study of the economy and appropriate decision-making has also spread to the business world and to the labour organizations. Business firms take great interest in the study of their share in the aggregate production of their industry and in the total national production. This interest is exhibited in a desire either to expand their part of the total production of their industry or to adapt their activity to that of other industries. They also find in the accounts factual data about the distribution of national expenditure, i.e. which markets are expanding and which are contracting.

For the labour organizations the income part of the accounts is of particular interest in decision making. Here they find the distribution of the shares of income and the correlation of these shares with production.

2. Though the international organizations have the ambitious aim of being able to use the national accounts for international comparisons of production and income, it has to be admitted that with the present vast economic and social differences between the various countries this must remain for some time no more than an ideal. However, serious attempts have been and could still be made to compare the production, income, consumption, and capital formation of countries in various parts of the world.

3. The accounts constitute a framework which makes possible a continuous systematically interrelated and consistent record of data on the basic economic functions in an economy – production, consumption, and accumulation of capital.

4. Because of the consistency of the accounts, it is possible to obtain some hitherto unavailable but required aggregates in the way of balancing residuals. This is particularly advantageous for developing countries where the collection of statistical data has not reached all branches of economic activity. This consistency also makes it possible to derive the various combinations of aggregates essential for economic analysis.

5. It is not uncommon to find that independent statistics compiled by various organizations and institutions, private or public, are biased to a greater or less degree according to the views or policies of the organizations. The simultaneous use of these data in the framework of the national accounts makes it possible to disclose and correct any errors or biases in statistics compiled in isolation.

6. The system has often been justly referred to as a meeting place for economic theory and practical possibilities. The possible as compared with the theoretically desirable classification of the various sectors of an economy, the grouping and aggregating of transactions, the application of various concepts, are all tested empirically. While some of these classifications and concepts fit in the system and thereby help further economic analysis, others are brought back to the economist for further consideration and classification of the problems involved.

7. The accounts provide primarily a quantitative description of the structure and economic activity of a country in a period of time. They become particularly useful when applied in aggregate econometric model building. The consistency of the accounts make it possible to indicate and forecast economic trends more precisely.

For most of these econometric models a series of national accounts over a long period of time is required.

It will later be demonstrated how the national accounts become a direct tool in forecasting economic activity and in economic programming and planning when used in combination with the input-output system.

8. The national accounts have also been found to be useful in the teaching of economics. Basic economic concepts and identities are grasped more easily and made clearer by following the inter-relationship between the various aggregates and accounts. Prominent economists have written textbooks using the national accounts approach as a pedagogical method for explaining and analyzing economic activity and interdependence.

9. National accounts could be very useful in the construction of periodical national balance sheets. Many important points of mutual interest to both systems could be brought to light.

II · SECTORING AN ECONOMY

Before proceeding with the description, and analysis of the national accounts system as recommended by international organizations and its comparison with those in use by some major and highly in-dustrialized countries, some of the basic concepts and definitions underlying this system will be clarified. Such a clarification may, indeed, throw light on the concepts of the other social accounting systems it is proposed to study. The first concept to be discussed is that of sectoring an economy for a national accounts system.

A variety of economic activitities are performed in each society. Innumerable transactions are carried out daily in the course of these varied activities. The whole population and its various organizations and institutions are involved in these transactions. They are the transactors. All these transactions, transactors and activities must be reduced to proportions which can be intelligibly grasped and analyzed. To achieve this, transactions must be classified by definite types, activities distinguished in form, and the transactors grouped into meaningful sectors. Moreover, the classification of transactions must be attributed to specific sectors.

No social accounting system, constructed as it is to give as concise as possible a presentation of the economic activity, should claim competence to embrace all aspects of economic and financial activity with similar thoroughness for the use of policy makers, or to supply all the empirical data for ramified economic and financial theories. A social accounting system is admissible as long as it has a coherently determined plan for the analytical presentation of economic aggregates, so that there is some interdependence between them. It is the interdependence and not the comprehensiveness that determines whether the set of accounts constitute a system or not. A certain aspect of economic or financial activity may be ignored by one system, and another sphere of productive activity may be disregarded by some other system. Each system, however, must, within its domain, show a coherent and distinct connexion between the various components of the flows included, the interrelationship between these flows, and the building up of the flows into aggregates. Furthermore, it cannot be argued that because one system is more suitable than another to the thorough analysis of a certain aspect of economic activity, therefore by amalgamation of the two systems an analytical tool could be constructed with which it would be possible to cope with all the economic problems of all the different economic structures. A comprehensive, interdependent, and articulated social accounting system must still remain an ideal.

Each social accounting system must, as will become more obvious later, have the economy sectorized according to the main task of economic or financial analysis it has been designed to perform. The way in which the economy is sectorized is indeed one of the clearest indicators of the major aims of a particular social accounting system. It will therefore be necessary to refer continuously to the sectoring problems of each social accounting system and to the sectoring approach of the various versions of each social accounting system.

The national accounts system has been regarded from its inception as a framework for describing and demonstrating the mutual relationship between production activity, income originating in production, and the use of the income for consumption and capital accumulation. The production, consumption, and saving functions in an economy are performed by various, but not necessarily different, transactors each performing one or more functions. The similarity of functions performed by the transactors is the criterion for their classification into sectors. A transactor who performs two different functions could then be grouped into two sectors. A farmer in his capacity as a farmowner is classified as belonging to the enterprize sector, while in his transactions as a consumer he is included in the households sector. While the functional division of the groups of transactors is the main consideration in sectoring for national accounts, the division is also approached – implicitly at least – from the point of view of the economic aims of the transactors. When a transactor performs a certain economic or financial function he does it generally with a definite aim in mind. We are all aware of the fact that the aims and motives of the private producers and sellers, or those of the owners of the productive factors in a modern industrialized monetary system, are different, if not opposed, to those of the 'have not' consumers. The government, on its part, may also have its decided aims and policies in the social economic, political, or military spheres of the society and its transactions are determined accordingly. Implicitly, then, the aims of the transactors are therefore also to be taken into consideration.

It should, however, be stressed again that the sectoring for the national account system is largely on a functional basis. Indeed any change in this basis is liable to put out of balance the whole structural framework and make it useless for the purpose for which it was originally constructed.

An economy, for most national accounts systems, is divided into three sectors. These three sectors are: the consumers' sector; the producers' sector; and the government sector. This classification concerns the sectoring of the domestic economy of a nation. But the economic and financial activity of a nation is not limited to the political boundaries of a country. It normally extends beyond its national boundaries. A detailed statement of these activities is presented in what may be regarded as the oldest and first social accounting system, viz. the balance of payments accounts. In the national accounts a separate summary account – rest of the world account – is allocated for these transactions. It should perhaps be remarked here that the principle of dividing economic and financial transactions into domestic transactions and international transactions can be usefully extended to a regional division of a country's economy.

Since, as already intimated, the author regards the sectoring of an economy as one of the fundamental cornerstones of a social accounting structure, more will be said about this in discussing the individual systems.

III · PRODUCTION BOUNDARIES

Economists hold different views as to what production is and what is its exact sphere. The differences are particularly sharp between those economists who follow the traditional principles of economics developed in the western world and those who adhere to socialist or Marxist economic doctrines. Since this study is mainly concerned with the social accounting systems used in the western world, it will suffice here to give the general definitions assumed in the western world. In the section on Soviet concepts of national income the difference in their approach will be briefly discussed.

A general definition of production for all social accounting systems would be the provision of goods and services. Such a definition would account for the provision of goods and services by one productive unit to another productive unit as well as the provision by the whole productive system of the final goods and services for final demands. A more restricted definition of production is any process by which new value is created or value is added to the value of goods already in existence. This definition is restricted in the sense that it involves the problem of value. It still remains a general definition in so far as it can be equally applied to accounting for interindustrial production as well as for accounting limited to final production of goods and services. But by introducing the problem of value this definition tends to limit the scope of production because it relates the concept of production to the interplay of the various forces in the economy which determine the value of goods and services. It comes to mean only that kind of production which can technically be measured in monetary terms. In a monetary market economy such a definition tends to become limited to that part of production which is reflected in the sales and purchases transactions of the market. The production of goods and services which do not for one reason or another reach the market and/or are difficult to evaluate in money terms, will not be regarded as falling within the sphere of production. Neither of these definitions, however, exactly describes production as actually applied to the social accounting systems. Some of the systems give the concept a wider meaning, whereas others narrow down its meaning. Production in the national accounts systems can be said to be limited to the production of final goods and services. This is in striking variance with the concept as applied in the input-output system, where the whole process of production is accounted for.

The sphere of production in both systems is expended by imputations. The degree of imputation differs from one system to another and also from one version of a national accounts system to another. In all cases, imputation is used to a limited degree. Arguments in support of this view will be given after the discussion of the concept of final goods and services, which are accounted for in the national accounts system, and of the concept of intermediate products, which are shown in an input-output table.

A. FINAL AND INTERMEDIATE PRODUCTS

When discussing the impact of business accounting on the national account system, it has already been stated that the technical accounting approach of the system is in some respects similar to that of the business accounting system of a large enterprise with many subsidiaries. The difference between the concept of a final product and that of an intermediate product could be made clear by following the procedure of consolidating the income accounts of a large concern consisting of several subsidiary companies. An accountant familiar with the accounts of such a large concern has a clear idea of how the income and expense accounts of the financial year are to be summed up for the concern. He knows that while he can add up or combine all those expenses which have been charged to the cost of production in each of the subsidiaries, he must not include the products which one subsidiary 'purchased' from, or 'sold' to the other sister company. Here he must consolidate instead of combining. He does this by cancelling out each of the 'purchases' (or 'sales') against the 'sales' (or 'purchases') of products to the sister factories. Those products which were 'purchased' (or 'sold') by one company from (or to) the other company of the same concern and charged to cost (credited to income) during the accounting period are the intermediate products. Those products, on the other hand, which were sold to outsiders by the head office of the concern, or by the individual subsidiaries, and/or those products which were charged to the inventory stock of each of these subsidiaries of the firm are the final product. A final product must not be taken to mean a finished product. Some of these final products may indeed still be in the form of raw materials (which might be the 'final' products of another firm), or goods in process.

It should also be added that any building construction, machinery, or other durable instrument, produced during the financial year by the companies for their own use, is also to be considered among the final products. These additions to the plant and equipment of the concern are regarded, by the same rule, as if the concern has sold to itself.

This technical approach of the accountant of a large firm leads to these compact general definitions of intermediate and final products. A product purchased and charged to cost by other producers at the same period is an intermediate product; whereas a product purchased and not charged to cost is a final product.

The discussion of the concept of intermediate and final products has so far been limited to the enterprise sector. Some of the points brought out may be of simple character when applied to non-financial enterprises. They do however raise some problems when applied to financial intermediaries. Neither the input nor the output of these institutions can be as simply defined and estimated as in the case of industrial enterprises. The problem of estimating production in financial intermediaries will be analyzed under the heading of imputations which is the next concept to be discussed.

A distinction between intermediate and final production in the government sector (not to be confused with the production of public enterprises which is included in the production of the enterprise sector) is also not easily made. A simple case is that of the government providing seeds or fertilizer to farmers who in their capacity as producers are included in the enterprise sector. These seeds and fertilizers might have been produced by government institutions as a by-product of their service operations. When given free of charge to farmers they can either be treated as final product of the government, or be considered as an intermediate product of the government by imputing to the production account a subsidy to farmers equal in value to the estimated expenditure on these seeds and fertilizers.

In most national accounts, final production is recognized also within the household sector. An example of such final production is the sale of domestic services of households to households. A production account is set up for the household sector out of which the services rendered within this sector are considered to be bought at cost, i.e. the account of the sector is debited and credited with the same amount.

B. IMPUTATIONS

The problem of whether services should or should not be considered as an integral part of production is connected with one of the basic differences between the economic thinking of the western economists and that of Marxian economists. Western economists generally hold the view that production is the utilization of scarce resources for the satisfaction of human wants which can be measured in monetary value. All the scarce resources, which in the view of the western economists generally consist of land, labour, capital, and entrepreneurship, take part in this process of satisfying human wants by providing goods as well as services which have a market value. Marxian economists, on the other hand, regard as production only the provision of material goods and consider that these material goods are produced by 'social labour' only, i.e. by that part of the labour force which takes part in the production of the material goods. It should be remarked that according to this last qualification, the services of a watchman or a cleaner of an enterprise producing material goods is also regarded as taking part in the production process. That part of the population which is not occupied in the production of material goods, i.e. those occupied in the providing of non-productive services, derive their income, according to Marxian thinking, from the redistributed income earned by social labour.

The analysis of the concept of imputations opened with the above cursory description of the difference in the general approach to the provision of services because the concept of imputation centres largely around the imputation of services. As the analysis of this concept proceeds it will be necessary to refer again to these differences in approach and their impact upon the applicaion of the concepts of imputation for national accounts purposes.

It will perhaps be convenient to start out with the purchase of domestic services by households from households mentioned in the last paragraph of the analysis of final and intermediate products, since this leads to the highly disputed subject of the services of housewives. In no national accounts system are the services of housewives imputed, though many social accountants hold the view that these services should be imputed as income originating. The housewife should be regarded as part of the nation's labour force which, particularly in an industrially developed country, is a scarce resource. There can be no difference between a woman who goes to work in an office or factory and hires domestic service and a housewife who does the work for her family. The argument that the activity of the members of a society must be divided into economic and non-economic activity cannot be applied here. A non-economic activity as the author would define it is a human activity which is of a recreational character or for which monetary value cannot possibly serve as a criterion for measurement. The services of the housewife are a non-market activity because their value is not directly determined by the market, but they are not a non-economic activity. There are in a society certain tasks that one or another member of the family will perform as his or her responsibility towards the family life. Helping a child to prepare his school work, for which teachers are not usually employed, is a clear example. The keeping of the garden around the house and other similar jobs would be, to a far from negligible extent, done by members of the family even if all of them were working outside as well. Only such activities are to be considered as non-economic activity performed in leisure time. Such tasks as driving of cars on family outings, are done for purely personal reasons, generally for the pleasure derived in doing them.

So far the problem has been examined with regard to an industrially developed country where labour is a scarce factor of production. In developing countries such imputations are justified on still other grounds. In such countries, the housewife not only performs the traditional jobs of the housewife in an industrially and/or socially developed country but also does other jobs such as baking the bread, bringing wood or other fuel for the cooking, or going to the market to sell domestically produced goods. The social status of the housewife is often such that practically all work in and outside the house is her job. It has therefore been claimed sometimes that for the sake of better international comparisons, at least for those tasks for which specialized industries exist in industrialized countries, such as bakeries and laundries, imputed income should be considered for housewives who perform such tasks themselves. This suggestion has been rejected on the grounds that it is statistically difficult to determine the extent and value of these services. The need to attach a value to the concept of production makes it at times technically difficult to account for a certain sphere of production.

The general reluctance to impute the services of the housewife appears to be based on the tacit view of the social accountants that the part of services in the measurement of national product should be kept at a minimum. This view follows apparently from some misinterpretation of the socialist approach to the provision of services. The socialist approach that services are not part of social production does not imply that there should be no accounting for them. It is only contended that services are not a social product and that the payment for them is derived from the productive income.

National accounts should bring out more explicitly the part of services in the total national product but at the same time include all services involving economic activity, whether market or non-market. It would for income analysis purposes be useful to know which part of the national product is increasing or decreasing; it is of major interest to know whether it is the part of the commodities produced that has increased or the part of the various services that has increased.

Gilbert and Kravis, after a thorough analysis of the problem of imputation based on their practical experience with countries of various degrees of social and economic development, recognize the fact that 'it is sometimes thought that it is essential to take a wider range of non-market activities into account to assure comparability in real product comparison, not only between advanced and under-developed countries, but between advanced countries themselves.' [20, p. 66]. But they nevertheless soon arrive at the conclusion 'that the useful limits of such extensions of the sphere of economic activity – as opposed to personal or non-economic activity – are quickly reached.' [20, p. 66]. In their view the limits are imposed: 1. By the practical fact that some non-market activities do not result in large enough production to be worth considering statistically; 2. By the necessity for analytical purposes of a distinction between economic activity and leisure-time activity; 3. By the fact that no quantitative measurement of the value of the whole of non-economic activity is possible because there is no way of weighing the value of one activity as against another'. [20, p. 66].

It would seem that some statistical study would be required to show that these 'non-market' activities are absolutely and relatively not worth considering. Non-market activities in an industrially developed country may perhaps be small in value as compared with other economic activities. But it would seem that their relative value in a developing country might be comparatively high.

The study would also have to determine that this holds true under normal conditions of peace time as well as during war or quasi war periods. Not an insignificant number of families have, during wars, grown their own vegetables or kept hens, etc., and this home production has then constituted an important contribution to agricultural production.

It is often of interest to many users of the national accounts to find out from the accounts to what extent production has shifted from real goods to services. It would also be of interest to determine the shifting of production from 'non-market' economic activity to 'market' economic activity. Such information would be of particular interest when periods of disturbance end and normal conditions obtain again.

It would, finally, have to consider the fact that what is a 'non-market' activity in a market economy can very well be a 'market' activity in a socialist country. A mother of a family in a non-socialist village, busy taking care of her children, is engaged in a 'non-market' activity. But the staff of a childrens' home in a kolkhoz, where the children are kept during the day, will be performing a 'market' activity, though a 'non-productive' one in a socialist state.

A great deal of 'non-market' activity may well be, as already pointed out, economic activity. There may be technical difficulties in estimating the value of these activities but the fact that the valuation is complicated cannot conceptually serve as a reason for considering them as non-economic activity. A 'leisure time' or recreational kind of activity, on the other hand, has nothing to do with an economic value criterion. A distinction should only be made between economic activity and 'recreational' activity.

c

The national accounts systems have in principle adopted the approach of Professor Pigou that 'just as economic welfare is that part of total welfare which can be brought directly or indirectly into relation with money measure, so the national dividend is that part of the objective income of the community, including, of course, income derived from abroad which can be measured in money.' [30, p. 31] It has however been applied with some hesitation and inconsistency. If the widest range of imputation were adopted, the problem of estimating the activity to be imputed could be overcome. All imputed income should, indeed, be clearly identified in the accounts.

A close and objective comparison of productivity between countries, and particularly between socially and economically developed countries and developing countries, and between capitalist and socialist countries, could not be successfully attempted before these problems would be solved.

But as things stand now, there is a rather long list of marginal, disputed cases which are solved by formed traditions and conventions of national income measurements, or for which specific but limiting rules were laid down by the international organizations in their effort to have comparable figures in national product and income. It would be useful to mention here some of these rules.

It has been a widely accepted rule to charge to factor income the food produced by farmers and consumed by themselves. It is this imputation that provoked the problem whether some other products produced by primary producers should be treated in a similar manner. A clear approach to this matter is important for comparison with developing countries. More about this problem of imputation will be said when the national accounts system as recommended by the United Nations is discussed.

Food given to workers by farmers, or coal given by coal mines to miners, are usually imputed in final product and charged to wages; but amenities to employees are charged to costs and not imputed in the same way. Or, conversely, transport provided by employers to bring the employee to the place of work is usually charged to cost, while the transportation expenses of the workers travelling on their own account is considered as a consumer expense on a final service. The procedure adopted in recording the amenities of employees and the bringing of employees to work follows the taxation regulations. It is the common practice of tax authorities to regard these expenditures as part of the cost of production or, in other words, not to levy taxes on these benefits to the employees. To add these costs to the compensation of employees in the national accounts would give an incorrect picture of the tax possibilities under the accepted tax regulations.

The question whether workers' expenses on transportation to work should be considered in the national accounts as final consumption, also often depends on the tax regulations. The solution therefore varies from one country to another. It would depend on whether these expenses are or are not deducted from the taxable income of the worker. Objectivity would prescribe that national accounts rules should not be related to any government regulations which are liable to be changed.

National accounts systems impute rent as factor income for houses occupied by their owners. Rent is also imputed for dwellings given by employers for the use of their employees. But housing accommodation for the armed forces or lodgings provided by an employer which is of no monetary benefit to the employee are not imputed in a similar way.

Of particular interest are the imputations of the services of the commercial banks, life insurance companies, and other financial intermediaries.

The major functions of the commercial banks are to accept deposits from the public and distribute these funds in the form of loans to their clients. Depositors, if charged at all, are charged small amounts for the keeping of their accounts. The income of the banks from such charges is relatively small, and in most cases would not cover the administrative expenses of the bank. In most cases, particularly in the case of fixed term deposits, the banks would pay some interest on the credit balances of the depositors. The main source of income for the banks is indeed the interest charges for the loans issued. Part of this interest received goes to cover the interest which the banks pay in most cases on the deposits of their depositors, while the rest is used for administrative expenses and the accumulation of profit. Since the interest earned is mainly on the money of the depositors and, since the exact cost of the bank's service, having no market price, cannot be easily determined, the share of the bank's contribution to domestic product is estimated as administrative expenses, such as salaries, rent, depreciation, and a certain profit margin. As indicated, almost no bank could cover all these costs by the actual service charges to depositors. The method generally adopted by the national accounts systems is therefore to charge the depositors – some of whom are households, while others are enterprises – with an additional imputed charge which is equal to the excess of the interest received from borrowers over the interest paid to depositors for their credit balances, plus all the operational expenses of the bank. The depositors would then be credited with an imputed receipt of interest on their deposits equal to the imputed additional charge for keeping their deposit accounts. Since the enterprise sector in which the banks (as we shall see later) are generally included, is credited, though not in the same account, with an imputed interest receipt equal to its share in the service charge on its proportion of the deposits with banks, the savings balance of the whole enterprise sector remains, in final analysis, unchanged. The households sector account is also left unchanged because against the imputed service charge on its deposits, it is credited with a similar amount as an imputed interest income. The gross domestic product is increased by the imputed service charge on the deposits of households.

Adopting the principle that interest paid by enterprises is a factor income emphasizes that the services of banks are of an intermediary character. Their factor charges are for their services as financial intermediaries. It does, however, complicate the problem of the proper presentation of bank accounts for national accounts purposes. Since the interest is the factor income of the creditors of the banks –

the depositors – and not that of the banks themselves, the banks are left with the small service charges which they actually collected. This leads to the paradoxical result that banks should show a loss whereas in fact they have proper margins of profit. An imputation for additional service charges is the only solution. It should however be admitted that the recommended method of imputation as described before is technically complicated and has its shortcomings. The shortcomings of this method of imputation are:

1. Banks will not always disclose the distribution of the deposits according to their owners. The allocation of the imputed service charge in proportion to the deposits of enterprises and the deposits of households must consequently be determined somewhat arbitrarily.

2. The imputed charges for services and the respective credit for interest are based on the deposit balances and not on the turnover of these deposits. The turnover in the deposit accounts of enterprises is normally larger than for personal deposit accounts. The imputed service cost to the enterprises should therefore be relatively larger than the imputed service cost to households. The compilation of the data on the turnover of the respective deposits involves, of course, still more difficulties.

3. No part of the service charge imputed is allocated to borrowers. The enterprises – borrowers of a bank may either be altogether different from the enterprises – depositors of the bank, or keep larger or smaller deposits in proportion to the amounts that they borrow from the bank. These two situations may also hold true with regard to the personal deposits and loans.

The case of life insurance companies is in some respects similar to that of the commercial banks. Life insurance companies perform two major functions. They insure against the death of the policy holder, who is usually the breadwinner of the family. They also serve as savings funds for the insured and they make investments out of these funds. The transactions between the companies and the policy-holders are not easily distinguishable because of this double function. Various policy holders pay various premiums for both of these services. The life insurance companies also receive interest on the investments made with the savings part of the premiums. On the other hand, they pay death claims to the beneficiaries of the insured and have to cover their operational expenses. The generally accepted imputation procedure is therefore to consider the receipts of premiums and payments of death claims as capital transfers between households. Since these transfers are within the households sector they are consequently disregarded. The income from the investments of the companies is considered as if actually disbursed to the policy-holders within the current year. The companies, to cover their administrative expenses, are then considered to charge the policy-holders for their services and in this they act in a way similar to the commercial banks. These imputed expenses are charged to the insured against the above income from investments imputed to their credit. More will be said about the imputations of the services of life insurance companies when examining those financial transactions accounts which are particularly concerned with financial intermediaries.

IV · CONSUMPTION AND CAPITAL FORMATION

Final products may be used for immediate consumption or be withheld for future use. The withholding of final products for future use constitutes the capital formation which is divided into fixed capital, increase in stock, and lending abroad.

These are very general definitions of the concepts of consumption and capital formation. The flow of consumption in national accounts is wider than the immediate consumption of goods and services by households and governments. Conversely, the fixed assets part of the capital formation aggregate is less than all the fixed assets added in a period of time.

Consumption of goods by households includes not only goods which for all practical purposes are immediately consumed by them but also all durables purchased except dwellings. Recording the purchase of durables as consumption may create in many instances, and under certain circumstances, a distorted picture of a nation's propensity to consume. A large number of consumers will buy a new durable commodity during the year in which it appears on the market but a smaller number will buy it during the following years. Increased immigration to a country, or the shifting of population from one area to another for political reasons, will usually result in unusual spending on durables. Purchases of durables in post-war periods are commonly larger than in normal times. All these changes would not be properly reflected in intertemporal and international comparisons. To include in consumption the purchase of yachts and aeroplanes for private use by a certain income group would also give an incorrect picture of the propensities to consume of the different income groups of the same country. It should however be admitted that durable commodities in the hands of the consumers are not productive in the same direct manner as are the capital assets of enterprises. In socialist thinking, durables are regarded as goods which are not socially disposable. Their services become restricted to their owners only. Durables are sometimes shown as a separate flow of consumption. Such a segregation is of great use not only in income analysis but also in financial analysis, because the purchase of durables is often financed by consumer credits whereas the purchase of other consumer goods is largely against cash.

Consumption of goods by governments (excluding government enterprises) as shown in national accounts could probably be better named absorption than consumption. It includes not only durables and inventories but also buildings and other constructions, though the degree of such inclusion varies, as will become evident later, from one system to another. The main conceptual reason for this procedure is that these capital assets are no longer within the productive circle. They are much akin in character to the durables in the hands of consumers. It may also be that social accountants have adopted this approach not only on the conceptual grounds mentioned but also because of the traditional government accounts system. Unlike the commercial accounts system, government accounts systems consist of revenues and disbursement accounts only. They do not contain asset accounts. All amounts spent, whether on current expenditures, or on capital goods, are recorded as disbursements. Generally speaking it can be said that considerations of political and/or military secrecy probably determine the presentation of government's consumption in the national accounts of a country.

The fixed assets of the capital formation aggregate as conceived by most of the national accounts systems consist of real assets such as machinery, buildings, and other constructions. This concept leaves out many expenditures such as advertising campaigns or research and development schemes which an individual enterprise might charge to non-tangible assets, such as goodwill or patents.

Another expenditure which is generally not shown by national accounts systems as part of capital formation is the wealth of knowledge acquired. The systems show all amounts spent on education as final services consumed. None of these expenditures are charged to the wealth of acquired knowledge. Even technical and other higher education costs are charged to consumption. Students engaged in higher studies are considered as engaged in non-economic activity. Students of institutions of higher learning are of a working age and therefore a factor resource. They could perform other activities generally accepted as economic activities. Their studies should therefore be imputed. In the case of housewives it is suggested that the amount to be imputed for the services rendered is to be charged to consumption expenditures, while in the case of students the imputed amount should be charged to capital formation.

Dwelling houses acquired by households for their own use or for letting out to others are considered as capital formation. These households, as will be seen later, are included in the enterprise sector in their capacity as houseowners and included in the households sector as consumers.

Capital formation also includes increases in stock. Stocks of goods are usually regarded by national accountants to consist of raw materials, goods in process, and finished goods with enterprises, grain, and livestock with farms and stockpiles of general government.

Lending is another component of capital formation. It is the balancing item in the capital account transactions of a nation with the rest of the world. Though the name indicates a positive balance, it can also be negative, i.e. borrowing of the nation from the rest of the world. It then appears as a negative figure. This may indeed be the case with the other components of capital formation. A nation may consume part of its capital assets.

V · GROSS VERSUS NET PRODUCTION

The term 'net' or 'net production' has, in fact, several meanings in the field of social accounting in the western world, and still another meaning in the socialistic national income accounts. The latter will be clarified when the USSR concepts of national income accounts are discussed, and in the section dealing with the input-output system. In national accounts it means the final production after having accounted for depreciation of the fixed capital used up in the process of production.

Fixed capital is used up by wear and tear in the process of production. Some of the equipment while still physically not worn out may have lost its value because of obsolescence, i.e. it cannot be used efficiently and competitively any more. Some accidental damage may have occurred in the course of production. For all these losses of wealth, provisions are usually set aside. The value of total production before these provisions are made is on a gross basis. The value of the total production after the provisions for the consumption of the fixed capital have been made is the net product. The provisions for the consumption of fixed assets is in a way similar to the netting out of the intermediate products when measuring final products.

In a dynamically growing economy, where the fixed capital is constantly changing in quantity and in quality or in technical construction, the method of estimating these provisions for 'keeping capital intact' are practically difficult and theoretically highly disputed. The general rule in national accounts is that the depreciation provisions should be estimated on a replacement basis. But in a business world where on one hand there are constant changes in prices, quantities, and technology, and where, on the other hand, the accounts of individual firms are constructed on different computations of depreciation, the application of this rule leaves many uncertainties. The margin of error in the estimates of the provision for consumption of fixed assets is liable to be significant. This is probably one of the reasons that in economic analysis gross product is more often used than net product.

It is generally accepted in national accounts that the obsolesence to be taken into account refers only to foreseen obsolesence. Unforeseen obsolescence is generally not considered in estimating the provisions for the consumption of fixed capital. Such obsolescence is regarded as capital loss at the time it occurs.

An individual business will also set aside in its accounts a reserve for the depletion of the natural resources owned and operated by it. National accounts systems do not, as a rule, include such charges in their provisions for estimates of the consumption of fixed assets. The estimates of consumption of fixed capital do of course provide for the depreciation of the constructions and equipment employed to make the natural resources available.

VI · MARKET PRICES AND FACTOR COSTS

Import and export taxes, excise duties and local rates comprise the main categories of indirect taxes paid to Government authorities. These taxes are in practice usually charged to business expenses and consequently are included in the market price.

On the other hand, Government makes grants to producers either in the form of direct current payments to producers or by covering the differences between the prices which government trading organizations pay for the goods purchased by them and the prices for which these are sold to the public. These grants are called subsidies and are usually defined as negative indirect taxes. They constitute by convention part of the factor incomes but are not included in the market prices. As a result of these indirect taxes and subsidies, national product and national expenditure can be valued either at market prices, i.e. prices which include the indirect taxes net of subsidies, or at factor cost, which excludes them.

The advantage of showing the national expenditure – consumption and domestic capital formation – at market prices, on the basis of which statistics are usually compiled, is that these are the prices which the final buyers actually pay, so that they are more meaningful for economic analysis. They are convenient in the study of trade cycles or in market research. If, on the other hand, the aim is to throw more light on the problem of allocation of resources, the valuation at factor cost is indeed preferable. The procedure of valuing the final product at factor cost is adopted in the classification of final output by industrial origin – a classification usually made separately as a subsidiary table to the national accounts.

VII · COST, MARKET, AND REPLACEMENT VALUATIONS

It has already been previously stated that final expenditures statistics are usually compiled on a market price basis. While the data on consumer goods so compiled involve no particular problem, difficulties do arise in the valuation of capital formation.

Two sources of gross additions to stocks in an enterprise are possible. One source is the purchase of stocks not yet put into the production process. These are valued at purchase price. The other source consists of the goods in various stages of production produced by the enterprise and intended to be put into further processing or sale by the enterprise. These additions of stocks are valued at current market prices or reproduction cost. Such a method of inventory movement valuation establishes an accounting according to which stock sold or put into further processing will be charged at an amount sufficient to replace it at current prices.

On the basis of the above methods of valuation, any construction by an enterprise for its own use should in national accounts be valued at cost. By valuing enterprise-owned constructions in this way, that part of the profit which an outside contractor would realize or the losses which he would sustain are omitted from the annual profits or losses of the economy. They may of course appear later in the production results of the enterprise.

When discussing the concept of net production it has been pointed out that the provision set aside for the depreciation of fixed assets is based on replacement valuation. It has also been indicated that the errors in the estimates are liable to be great. Practically the same difficulties are encountered in the evaluation of the increase in stocks, because the methods adopted by individual firms for recording the movement of stock are far from being uniform. Some national accounts systems indicate in the accounts the difference between the replacement value of the increase in stocks and the 'book' value as found in the original sources of business accounting. It would be wise here to elucidate these differences.

Two methods of valuation of the use of stock are popular in the field of business accounting: the 'first-in-first-out' (fifo) method; and the 'last-in-first-out' (lifo) method. According to the 'fifo' method, inventories are charged out to production in the order of their acquisition, whereas according to the 'lifo' method materials acquired last are charged out first. Business accounts differ in their computations of these stock movements. If a few numerical examples are calculated the national accounts method of evaluation will be seen to be fairly similar to the 'lifo' method in times of physically increasing stocks, but only close to the 'lifo' valuation when stocks are physically decreasing. The 'fifo' method of evaluation will be close to that of the national accounts method in time of decreasing stocks and decreasing prices. All methods of evaluation will be similar to the national accounts method in times of stable prices.

Data on the extent and the rate of the increases in stock are of great value in the analysis of demand and market prices. The piling up or depletion of stocks held by enterprises are important economic indicators. It would therefore be very helpful to have reliable estimates of stock movement. National accountants of several industrialized countries, however, admit that these estimates are subject to a fairly wide margin of error.

VIII · CURRENT AND CAPITAL TRANSFERS, LENDING AND BORROWING

By transfers we generally mean unilateral payments made by a payer against no specific consideration from the recipient. Some of these transfers are more of the character of financial transactions – if they can be considered as transactions at all. Such transfers, examples of which will follow, may be called simple transfers. The person or group of persons receiving such transfers is not rendering any service or providing any product or involving itself in a financial counterclaim in return for this income. The transfers are made voluntarily by the transferors and mainly for specific persons or institutions in whom they take interest. They do not generally have in mind any general welfare considerations. Other transfers which are not formally listed under the name of transfers consist mainly of payments made by enterprises and households to government and vice versa. The transferees of such transfers receive this income for no *specific* service rendered *directly* to the transferors. The transferors are, generally speaking, forced to make these payments. They constitute an appropriation or redistribution of income which public policy deems necessary for the general welfare and security of the whole society.

Some national accounts systems have, for reasons indicated below, seen fit to differentiate between current transfers and capital transfers because of their different effect on the nation's economy.

Under current transfers are included subsidies from government authorities to enterprise and, in the opposite direction, indirect taxes from enterprises to the government. Current transfers from governments to households include grants for education, health, war bonuses, pensions, etc. The flow of current transfers from households to the government authorities include personal taxes and other transfers such as payments of school fees not classified in the accepted classification of consumption, driving tests, etc. Business allowances for bad debts are sometimes considered as current transfers from business to households. All these transfers have their influence upon consumption and market prices and bring about directly and indirectly change and re-distribution in the balance of savings of the different sectors of the economy. They are therefore recorded in the current accounts of the sectors.

Capital levies of all sorts including death duties etc., on enterprises and persons, confiscations etc., are viewed as capital transfers to the government. Flows in the opposite direction are grants for investments, war damages, etc., made by the government authorities to enterprises and households. Reparations, economic aid, and transfers of migrants are examples of capital transfers to and from abroad. Domestic capital levies, i.e. capital transfers between the sectors of the economy could in a way be regarded as capital gains and losses and, similar to the treatment of the latter, not be included in the accounts. However, these transfers, particularly those from abroad, affect the level of capital formation and the intra-sectorial change in the ownership of the capital. They have also been playing an important role in the economic policy of government in the course of the last two decades. They are therefore entered separately from current transfers, in the standard accounts of several countries.

A distinction between current transfers and capital transfers is, as indicated above, useful in economic analysis. The neatness of this differentiation gives a clearer indication of the composition of the current income of households and current revenues of the government, and how they have disposed of them. It also aids in the analysis of the savings capital provisions and other capital receipts which are used for the financing of capital formation. In practice, however, it is often difficult to implement this classification of transfers. The main difficulty lies in the fact that a transfer which from the point of view of the transferor is regarded as a capital transfer, may be regarded by the transferee as a current transfer, and vice versa. These difficulties are particularly common in transfers between the government and households. A payment by government of a lump sum to an individual in the way of, say, damages for a house demolished for some reason by the government, can be regarded as a current transfer if it was paid out of the current budget.

To the individual it is a capital transfer to be used for a capital investment – the construction of a new house.

A divergence in the treatment of transfers in the accounts of the transferors and transferees is of course liable to disturb the equality between savings and investments.

The impact of intersectorial borrowings and lendings on capital formation is similar to that of capital transfers between sectors. The borrowings and lendings within the country, like all domestic current and capital transfers, cancel out one against another. They do not contribute to the total finance of domestic capital formation. They do, however, shift from one sector to another the holding and operating of the nation's wealth. Borrowing from abroad, on the other hand, is an additional source of financing domestic capital formation; while lending to foreign countries is another form of investment. All national accounts systems have, therefore, found it convenient to include to varying extents such 'financial' transactions between the sectors of the economy and with the rest of the world.

IX · DOMESTIC AND NATIONAL CONCEPTS

An analysis of these concepts should be preceded by the following short definitions of two of the basic terms used. These are: (a) domestic territory and (b) resident. These terms are generally defined as in the balance of payments manual of the International Monetary Fund [23]. The third edition of this manual has been drawn up with a special effort to conform with the concepts and definitions of the national accounts as recommended by the United Nations and by the OEEC.

Domestic territory is broadly defined to include not only the territory within the country's political frontiers, but also ships and aircraft wherever they may be (as long as they are operated by domestic carriers) but excluding overseas territories and possessions.

The term 'resident' refers to individuals as well as to institutions. Resident individuals are individuals residing permanently and having their centre of interest in a given country. Tourists or commercial travellers travelling abroad, members of the diplomatic services, official missions, and armed forces stationed abroad are nevertheless considered residents; whereas citizens of a given country residing abroad are not. Resident institutions include all central and local governments and their agencies abroad, all business enterprises, and non-profit organizations located in a country. Branches or subsidiaries of resident enterprises, and intergovernmental organizations other than those engaged in non-financial activity are excluded.

In light of the above definitions it becomes clear that a consolidation of the production of all resident and non-resident producers in a domestic territory would result in a domestic product aggregate. This would be a pure domestic product aggregate. However, the domestic product aggregate as usually conceived in national accounts is one that excludes the product of non-resident producers in the domestic territory, termed by G. Stuvel [35] 'domestic imports' and includes the product of resident producers in non-domestic territory, called by Dr Stuvel 'domestic exports'.

The national product aggregate as conceived in national accounts is arrived at by adding to the domestic product the factor income earned by residents abroad and deducting the factor income of non-residents.

The domestic consumption aggregate consists of all the goods and services consumed by residents within the domestic territory. Residents also consume goods and services when visiting abroad, while non-residents consume goods and services supplied to them by the country they temporarily visit. By adding to the domestic consumption the consumption of residents abroad and deducting the goods and services supplied to non-residents we arrive at the total national consumption.

As a sequence to the term 'domestic imports' and 'domestic exports' the terms 'national imports' and 'national exports' have been suggested. National imports would cover, in addition to domestic imports, all factor income to non-residents and the consumption abroad by residents. National exports would consist of 'domestic exports', factor income from abroad to residents, and consumption expenditures of non-residents in the domestic territory.

It would probably be of interest for several western industrially developed countries where there has recently been an increase in 'domestic imports' and 'domestic exports' to have these figures shown separately. Such data could be shown in supporting tables to the standard accounts.

Fixed capital formation as conceived by national accounts consists of all fixed capital formed in the domestic teritory. Buildings and other constructions erected abroad, pipelines or machinery exported and installed abroad, whether operated by residents or non-residents, are considered as financial investments abroad. Fixed capital formation is a purely domestic concept because only the fixed capital added in the domestic territory is taken into account.

Increase in stock, on the other hand, could theoretically be divided into domestic increases and national increases. However, unlike fixed capital, increases in stock held abroad are regarded in national accounts as an increase in stock in the domestic territory and not as a financial investment abroad.

Fixed capital formation and increase in stocks both constitute domestic capital formation. By adding to these two components of capital formation all loans to the rest of the world which, as indicated above, includes also the countervalue of the fixed capital formed abroad, we obtain a national capital formation aggregate.

X · RECEIVABLE VERSUS CASH BASIS

More often than not business firms sell and buy on credit terms. But even in those cases where the sales are made against no credit there may elapse some short time between the delivery of goods and the receipt of payment. The usual commercial accounting procedure in all these cases is that as soon as the goods are transferred to the buyer, the latter is being charged with the agreed value. A 'receivable' is thereby being created in the records of the seller in lieu of real goods sold. The creation of receivables (or 'payables' from the point of view of the purchaser) is not limited to the sale of goods. It is also

D

prevalent in the accounting of services rendered. Services of various sorts may be supplied for which the actual cash payment is sometimes paid afterwards. Though there are some exceptions, particularly in the services provided by the liberal professions, the generally accepted method in business accounting is to charge the receiver of the services (or credit the supplier of the services) with the amount due for these services, pending the receipt of the actual payment. The opposite of the 'receivable payable' method is the method of recording the service rendered only as and when cash payment is made. This is known as the 'cash basis'.

Since national accounts systems are planned to show the real production and actual sales of goods and services, the accepted principle is, therefore, to record transactions on a receivable-payable basis which makes production invariant to financial arrangements. The implementation of this principle is facilitated by the fact that statistics of production and sales can be and usually are obtained on the basis of the actual output and the transfer of goods and services irrespective of the financial arrangements made, and consequently can be recorded on a receivable-payable basis. There is, of course, also the advantage that the required statistical data are in accordance with the methods generally applied in business accounts.

There are some instances where adjustments have to be made or where some special problems do arise. The accounts of public authorities, for instance, are usually kept on a cash basis and therefore require some adjustments before they can be used for national accounts purposes.

Practical difficulties arise in connexion with the estimating of obligations due to and from government authorities. An outstanding example is the problem of income tax estimates. Income tax is generally assessed on the basis of the income earned during the year prior to the year of assessment, and collected during the year following the year of assessment. The usual procedure of recording all receivables of income tax as well as other direct and indirect taxes in the national accounts is to consider these taxes as due at the time they are due to be paid without penalty.

Other practical difficulties are encountered in the compilation of import and export statistics. The statistics available are not gathered on the receivable-payable basis. They hardly could be. The statistics of imports and exports can conveniently be compiled on the basis of all the completed formalities for their admission to or exit from the country. These records also need to be adjusted if they are to be used for national accounts purposes.

XI · THE BASIC ACCOUNTING STRUCTURE

In the analysis of the concepts and definitions hitherto made, it has first been shown that the national accounts system is mainly oriented towards the systematic presentation of the three major forms of economic activity, viz. production, consumption, and capital accumulation. It has been indicated that the national accounts are limited to final production and consumption and the boundaries have been pointed out. It has also been indicated that, in view of the direct and indirect impact which current and capital transfers as well as borrowing and lending have upon the consumption and capital formation of the nation as a whole, and more particularly on the individual sectors, the national accounts systems have found it convenient to include these redistributive transactions into the accounting system.

The basic accounting structure for national accounts systems provides for each sector three accounts corresponding to each of the three major economic activities, and an additional account in which the sector's transactions with all the other sectors are recorded.

The first of these accounts is the production account which shows the revenue and expenses of the productive activity. On the debit side of this account are production expenses. These expenses mainly consist of the cost of materials bought from other sectors, the value of the materials produced by the sector for its own use, indirect taxes, and provisions for the consumption of the fixed capital used in production. On the credit side of the account are recorded the sales of consumption and capital goods – including the goods produced for own use – the increases of stocks, and subsidies received. The account is balanced out by the net value added by the sector.

This balance appears on the debit side of the production account and on the credit side of the appropriation account, the second mentioned, thus interlocking the two.

The net value added by the sector is equal to the factor income generated in the sector from its productive activity. The factor income consists of compensation of employees, interest, net rent, and operating profit. In addition to the factor income, there are also, on the credit side of the appropriation account, all the current transfers received from the other sectors including those from abroad, and income from investments. On the debit side of the account are first recorded all the current disbursements such as consumption, income payments, direct taxation, and current transfers to other sectors. The last item on the debit side is the saving of the sector. This is the balancing amount of the appropriation account which is transferred to the credit side of the third account – the capital account. Saving is the link between the appropriation account and the capital account.

In addition to the saving item which appears on the credit side of the capital account there are also recorded the provisions set aside for the consumption of the fixed capital employed by the sector. These provisions appear on the debit side of the production account. The other entries on the credit side of the capital account are the capital transfers and borrowings from other domestic sectors and from abroad. The debit side of the account shows the domestic capital formation (fixed capital and increases of stocks), the capital transfers made by the sector and its lendings to other sectors and foreign countries.

The fourth account, named the external account, closes the circle of the economic activity of the sector. As such it records on its debit side all those items which are shown on the credit side of the other accounts, and are not also shown on the debit side in one of the other accounts. On its credit side there are entered all items shown on the debit side of the other accounts and not also shown on the credit side in one of the other accounts.

Since the accounts of the basic accounting structure for each sector are interrelated and fully articulated, they can be expressed in a matrix form as shown on the following page.

An appendix at the end of this section illustrates in a usual accounting form the above basic accounting structure for each sector. It contains also hypothetical figures. Cross references are given to indicate how the various items in the four accounts are interlocked.

By combining the basic accounts of all the sectors of an economy only a sectoral, disaggregative picture of economic activity is obtained.

Credit / Debit	Production account	Appropriation account	Capital account	External account
Production account			Sales of capital goods Increase in stocks	Sales of consumers' goods Subsidies
Appropriation account	Net value added			Income from investments Current transfers from others
Capital account	Provisions for consumption of fixed capital	Saving		Capital transfers from others Borrowing
External account	Materials purchased Materials produced for own use Indirect taxes	Consumption Income payments Direct taxes Current transfers to others	Capital transfers to others Lending	

Appendix to Chapter One

BASIC ACCOUNTING STRUCTURE FOR A SECTOR

I. *Production Account*

	£		£
1. Materials purchased (IV, 7)	50	6. Sales of consumers goods (IV, 1)	76
2. Materials produced for own use (IV, 8)	5	7. Sales of capital goods (III, 1)	24
3. Indirect taxes (IV, 9)	10	8. Increase in stocks (III, 2)	8
4. Provisions for consumption of fixed capital (III, 6)	10	9. Subsidies (IV, 2)	12
5. Net value added = factor income generated by sector = compensation of employees + operating surplus (Interest, net rent and operating profit) (II, 6)	45		
	120		120

II. *Appropriation Account*

	£		£
1. Consumption (IV, 10)	30	6. Net value added (I, 5)	45
2. Direct taxes (IV, 11)	2	7. Income from investments (IV, 3)	5
3. Current transfers to others (IV, 12)	2	8. Current transfers from others (IV, 4)	5
4. Income payments (IV, 13)	3		
5. Saving (III, 5)	18		
	55		55

III. *Capital Account*

	£			£
1. Capital goods acquired (I, 7)	24	5. Savings (II, 5)		18
2. Increase of stocks (I, 8)	8	6. Provisions for consump- of fixed capital (I, 4)		10
3. Capital transfers to others (IV, 14)	4	7. Capital transfers from others (IV, 5)		5
4. Lending (IV, 15)	3	8. Borrowing (IV, 6)		6
	39			39

IV. *External Account*

	£			£
1. Sales of consumers goods (I, 6)	76	7. Materials purchased (I, 1)		50
2. Subsidies (I, 9)	12	8. Materials produced for own use (I, 2)		5
3. Income from investments (II, 7)	5	9. Indirect taxes (I, 3)		10
4. Current transfers from others (II, 8)	5	10. Consumption (II, 1)		30
5. Capital transfers from others (III, 7)	5	11. Direct taxes (II, 2)		2
6. Borrowing (III, 8)	6	12. Current transfers to others (II, 3)		2
		13. Income payments (II, 4)		3
		14. Capital transfers to others (III, 3)		4
		15. Lending (III, 4)		3
	109			109

CHAPTER TWO

A Comparison of
National Accounts Systems

I · UNITED NATIONS SYSTEM OF NATIONAL ACCOUNTS

After having reviewed in broad terms the basic concepts of the national accounts systems, it will now be shown how these concepts are applied in the national accounts systems as recommended by international organizations and by some industrially developed countries.

Special attention will be given to the structure of the standard accounts of each national accounts system. The analysis of most of the concepts will in effect coincide in most cases with the discussion of these accounts.

In practically all national accounts systems, the standard accounts of the system are supplemented by tables. These tables throw a different light on the various aggregates presented in the standard accounts. Only occasional reference will be made to these tables.

It will be convenient to begin with the description of the national accounts system as recommended by the statistical office of the United Nations [40]. This system became known among social accountants as SNA. This abbreviation will also be used here. SNA is a sequel to the earlier recommendations of the United Nations [39], previously mentioned. The earlier, as well as the present, system was drawn up by an international group of experts from western countries and is consequently constructed on the lines of western thinking.

A. THE SECTORS

The way a social accounting system classifies the transactors of an economy is probably the best reflection of its main aims and how it plans to achieve them. A detailed examination of how SNA sectorizes an economy is therefore of primary interest. It is only after such an examination that the *raison d'être* of most of the flows and aggregates presented in the standard accounts and tables is likely to become evident.

SNA divides the economy into three domestic sectors: enterprises; households, and private non-profit institutions; and general government. In addition to these three domestic sectors there is an account for transactions with all foreign countries – the rest of the world. Though the rest of the world account is frequently referred to as a sector, it should be emphasized that it is only an account in which the transactions of the domestic sectors with the whole world are recorded. The term 'sector' as used in national accounts implies a group of domestic transactors who behave in an economically similar manner, who affect, and are affected by, the other domestic sectors of the economy, and are mutually dependent one upon another. It also implies that the whole range of its production, consumption and capital formation are recorded in the national accounts. This is not the case with the rest of the world account. What is recorded in this account is no more than that part of economic activities where the domestic sectors come in contact with the rest of the world.

The SNA classification of the transactors into the three domestic sectors rests mainly on a functional basis. The functions of most of the transactors are clearly recognisable and the transactors performing these functions can be easily classified into the appropriate sectors. There are, however, some transactors whose functions are not so clearly distinguishable or who perform more than one function. A general outline of the transactors included in the three sectors of SNA will therefore be given. The outline will also serve as a basis for the comparison of the SNA sectoring methods with those of the other national accounts.

1. Enterprises. This is the sector which employs most of the factors of production. The transactors included in this sector are:

1. Private corporations and co-operatives providing the various goods and services. It should be pointed out that SNA includes in this group of enterprises banks, insurance companies, and similar financial intermediaries, as mere producers of services.

2. Unincorporated private enterprises which are defined to include farms, retail shops, craftsmen and professional men. Some of these transactors may be employing themselves only. The distinction between these enterprises and individual employees (included in the households, etc. sector) is that the latter provide a factor – labour service, while the former sell a good or a 'non-factor' service.

Typical of the other transactors which are included in this sector, (although only some of their functions are characteristic to this sector), are: households and private non-profit institutions in their capacity as owners of dwellings whether or not they occupy those dwellings; non-profit institutions founded by particular enterprises with the aim of having their earning capacity increased; and public enterprises, i.e. enterprises which are owned or controlled by public authorities. There are no steadfast rules by which public enterprises can be recognised and differentiated from private corporations. Some public enterprises are clearly identified, as, for instance, all the nationalized industries of a country, or the post office. Others might provide services often provided by private enterprise. These would however run on a wide scale and would be independent of the government departments they serve. Examples of such public enterprises are munition factories, repair shops for motor vehicles, and navy dock yards. Public hospitals and schools are not included among public enterprises.

SNA considers it convenient for certain analytical purposes to sub-divide public enterprises. (1) There are government enterprises usually defined as government agencies, financially integrated with general government and keeping only a few working balances, and (2) public corporations recognised generally by the fact that the government hold a predominant part of the corporation's shares, and more specifically identified as those bodies where the government has '... an effective influence in all the main aspects of management and not merely such influence as is derived from the use of public regulatory powers of a general kind' [40, p. 11]. The above sub-division of public enterprises may indeed be helpful. A complete segregation of the production of the whole public enterprise group from the production of the private enterprise group would have been better. The reasons for such segregation are twofold.

Private corporations and co-operatives and all unincorporated private enterprises are based on private initiative and are purely profit-seeking institutions. Public enterprises, on the other hand, are not oriented towards a maximization of profits. Public corporations may be trying their best to gain profits, but for government enterprises (the first part of the public enterprise group) this is normally a secondary consideration. There is one aspect of the working methods of private enterprises which should be stressed here, viz. that such enterprises will usually not take upon themselves the development of a new industry or a new region where there is more than the normal risk of losses. To show in one aggregate the production of the private and the public enterprises is therefore a particular shortcoming for the income analysis of developing countries.

While in most western countries the product of public enterprises may not constitute an important part of the total of national product, there are some countries where the part of the public enterprise product in the national product is constantly growing. In both cases these enterprises, as indicated before, often produce goods and services which perhaps might not otherwise have been produced at all or would have been produced at a larger cost to the individual consumer. It is therefore important for public policy decision to distinguish between the production of private enterprises and public enterprises.

Such a segregation would require clear and accepted standards by which public corporations would be distinguished from private corporations. A public corporation would be considered as such if (a) its shares are wholly or mainly owned by the government, (b) most of its long term liabilities are due to the government, (c) its management is appointed by government, (d) its sphere of production is one not commonly undertaken by private enterprise, (e) its main motive is not profit making.

Though it would be convenient for economic analysis to have within the standard accounts an additional sector for public enterprises, this is not recommended because standard national accounts should in general be limited to the minimum and be as compact as possible. The compactness of national accounts is one of their greatest advantages for general economic policy decisions. It would however seem advisable for the supporting Table II of SNA showing the industrial origin of gross domestic product at factor cost to have two columns in which the product of private enterprise and that of the public enterprises would be shown separately. The total of both columns will be the aggregate for the standard accounts.

ii. Households and private non-profit institutions. The word 'households' is generally used to mean the consuming public; that is to say all the 'residents' of a country, who are the immediate or final receivers of factor income, and at the same time the final consumers of products and services. The criterion of homogeneity in behaviour is indeed somewhat overstretched here. The behaviour of a household dependant on a low wage earner is different from that of the household of a rentier with a large income, or from that of a household whose head is for some reason not engaged in any productive activity. The function attributed to households is to receive factor income (or in some cases, and in certain periods of time, to receive 'transfers' from their own sector and/or other sectors) and to consume goods and services. But their incomes are not equal and neither are their consumptions absolutely and relatively equal. The propensities to consume (or the propensities to save) of the lower income groups are not the same as those of the higher income groups. By grouping all households into one sector, important data is kept from all those interested in the measurement of these propensities.

Private non-profit institutions are those institutions which are primarily organised neither with the aim of earning profits nor for the rendering of services to enterprises. These institutions may be in the legal form of corporations or associations, or of clubs or foundations. The most outstanding examples in practically all countries are the trade unions, the charitable societies, and certain private hospitals, schools, and universities. It is mainly because the activities of such non-profit institutions in serving households cannot be isolated from the functions of the households themselves that these institutions are combined with the households to make one sector. Where non-profit institutions have been established mainly for furthering the efficiency and profitability of enterprises, SNA recommends to include them in the enterprise sector.

It should be specially pointed out that according to SNA pension funds established by enterprises or governments for their employees are also to be included in the households sector. The functions of these funds are to provide financial services. But unlike the other financial intermediaries, which provide financial services to all sectors of the economy, the pension funds provide financial services to a specific group of the households sector alone. The savings of the households held by these funds would be shown directly as the savings of households. Were the pension funds included among the financial intermediaries, these savings would have to be transferred to the households sector by imputation, as for life insurance companies.

iii. General government. As 'public enterprises' are grouped in the enterprise sector, there is no special difficulty in the definition of the government sector by its functions. SNA defines the functions of general government as follows: 'The function of general government is to organise for, but not normally to sell to, the community those common services which cannot otherwise conveniently and economically be provided and to act as the administrative agency for the economic and social policy of the community' [40, p. 11].

For the supporting tables, SNA recommends a sub-division of this sector by type of authority as follows: (1) central government (2) state government (3) local authorities (4) social security funds excluding pension funds. SNA considers a social security fund as part of a general government sector if it serves as an instrument of the social policy of the government, i.e. only when it is imposed by government and the contribution to it by employers and/or employees is made compulsory. Where no such contributions are made but the fund is supervised, regulated, and greatly subsidised by Government, it should also be included in the general government sector.

B. STRUCTURE OF THE STANDARD ACCOUNTS

The entries in the basic accounts for each sector as described earlier in Chapter I provide practically all the raw data required for the national accounts system. It has, however, been found expedient to rearrange the data of the basic accounts in a set named 'Standard Accounts'. Some of these standard accounts are constructed so that the important and familiar general aggregates – such as 'gross national product', 'domestic product', 'national income', etc. are distinctly brought out.

In addition to these aggregate accounts there are also standard accounts for the households sector, for the government sector, and for the rest of the world. The arrangement of the standard accounts is aimed at helping various decision-making units in obtaining a general picture of that sphere of economic activity in which they take special interest. They are convenient to the economist in the analysis and study of the economic activity of a nation. The structure of the standard accounts is particularly convenient to policy-making bodies because of its compactness. The transposition of the flow from the basic accounts into the standard accounts could be manipulated in various ways to suit the needs of decision-making units and the analytical needs of the economist.

SNA standard accounts consist of the following six accounts: account (1) domestic product; account (2) national income; account (3) domestic capital formation (these are the aggregative accounts); account (4) households and private non-profit institutions; account (5) general government; and account (6) external transaction (rest of the world account). The last three accounts are each sub-divided into two: a current account, and a capital reconciliation account.

Appendix 'A' at the end of this chapter reproduces these six accounts. Hypothetical figures have been added for clear exposition of their interdependence. Because SNA standard accounts show borrowing and lending flows the system is not fully articulated. The accounts cannot, as they stand, be presented in a chessboard matrix form.

Account 1 of the standard accounts is an obvious statistical presentation of the Keynesian fundamental identity: $Y = C + I$, i.e., the income of the factors of production is identical with the consumer's expenditure on commodities plus the capital expenditure on real assets. The debit side total of the account gives the aggregate of gross domestic product at market prices, whereas the credit side shows the part of the product consumed and the part left as real assets accumulated during the reported period. Attention should be drawn to the fact that no transfers to and from abroad are included in this account any more than they are in the Keynesian identity.

The aggregate *net domestic product at factor cost* (NDP_f) on the debit side of the account is doubly net. It is net because it shows only the final production – the value added – of the economy, i.e., intermediate goods are netted out. This is in accordance with the basic structure and conceptual approach of the national accounts systems. It is also net in the sense that provisions for the consumption of the fixed capital used in production have been deducted.

The second item on the debit side of account 1 is *provisions for domestic fixed capital consumption* (D). According to SNA these provisions are to defray the current cost of wear and tear, foreseen obsolescence (but not unforeseen obsolescence, which is to be considered as capital loss at the time it occurs) and accidental damage to fixed capital. In other words the provisions to be made are those which are believed to be sufficient to cover the cost of replacing the fixed capital consumed in various ways during the period under report.

Several methods of computing the depreciation of fixed assets are used in business firms. However, only two methods, other than the replacement method, are of special interest here or later. There is first the method by which firms provide for the depreciation of their fixed assets on a straight-line basis. The original cost of each of the different fixed assets of the firm, is, according to this method, distributed over the expected lifetime of the corresponding item of fixed assets. This method of computation results in provisions which, under conditions of continuous rising prices and technological changes are much lower than in the replacement method recommended by SNA. The second widely used method provides for the depreciation of the fixed assets on a cumulative replacement basis. According to this method not only the current costs of the fixed assets consumed during the period under report are taken into account, but also the difference between the provisions made during the previous years for the consumption of the existing fixed assets on the basis of the then prevailing prices and the provisions required on the basis of the current prices. This method of computation leads obviously to provisions which, under conditions of increasing prices, are higher than the provisions on a replacement basis for the year under report alone. National accountants cannot therefore use the depreciation figures of business firms.

Because natural resources do not originate in production, SNA does not recommend provisions for the depletion of natural resources. It does recommend the provision for consumption of machinery and other fixed assets used for the discovery of these resources.

A total of the two flows viz. (NDP_f) and (D) discussed above would give us the gross domestic product at factor cost. Since Expenditures on consumption and on domestic capital formation by households and government, shown on the credit side of account 1, are more conveniently compiled on a market prices basis, and because market prices are in any case important for the study of price levels, the debit side of account 1, therefore, also contains the indirect taxes less subsidies items as defined below. By adding these latter flows to the two flows mentioned above, the gross domestic product at market price aggregate is produced.

Indirect taxes (*TI*) are generally identified either in that they are chargeable to business expenses, or in that they are levied upon the possession or use of goods and services by households. They are composed of import, export, and excise duties, local rates, sales taxes, motor vehicle duties, taxes on the operation of wireless and television sets, etc. SNA also recommends the treating of real estate and land taxes as indirect taxes except where these taxes are no more than an administrative device for the collection of income tax.

SNA does not consider the operating surpluses (interest, net rent, and operating profits) of state monopolies as a gain from production activity but as an indirect tax. This treatment of the operating surpluses of state monopolies does not affect the aggregate of the gross domestic product at market prices but it does reduce the figure of the domestic product at factor cost.

Subsidies (*SU*) are an expenditure flow and therefore a debit entry on the general government current account. This item should have consequently appeared as a credit entry in the domestic product account. But as it was desired to bring out the aggregate of gross domestic product at market prices, it is shown on the debit side of account 1 with a minus sign. This also brings out the fact that subsidies are regarded as negative indirect taxes.

SNA views all current grants by general government in the production sphere – whether made directly to producers, or in the form of a differential between the buying and selling prices of government trading organisations – as subsidies. Regarding all government grants to producers as subsidies, and considering the operating surpluses of state monopolies as indirect taxes leads logically to another SNA recommendation. This recommends that grants made to public enterprises which constantly incur losses should be included among subsidies rather than deducting the operating deficits from the

E

operating profits of enterprises. When analysing the SNA sectoring it was argued that public enterprise production should be segregated from that of the private enterprise. It may now be added that after such segregation it would become meaningful to show subsidies to private public enterprises separately.

The first flow on the credit side of account 1 is *private consumption expenditure* (C_h). Included in this flow are the final expenditures – actual and imputed – of households and private non-profit institutions on current goods and services, less the proceeds from the sale of second-hand goods, plus the value of gifts in kind received from abroad, minus the value of gifts in kind sent abroad, plus expenditures of residents abroad, less expenditures of non-residents in the domestic territory.

As already indicated when analysing the basic concepts, most of the national accounts systems include in this flow all goods of whatever durability except buildings. The SNA flow of private consumption follows the same line and includes all consumer durable goods with the exception of land and buildings purchased by housholds and non-profit institutions. SNA, which was constructed to provide better international comparisons of economic activity, including developed as well as developing economies, should have recommended that the private consumption expenditures on durable consumer goods be shown as a separate flow in the standard accounts. The main arguments for a separate flow for the private consumption of durables were given earlier. Another argument may now be added. SNA, aiming for international comparisons, should have taken into account the fact that any rise in economic activity in developing countries, resulting as it will in a rise in the general standard of living, is bound to cause heavier spending on durable consumer goods. Durables purchased by households in developing countries are also likely to be serviceable in nature, whereas a significant amount of those bought by the more developed countries are likely to be stylish rather than functional. A separate flow within the standard accounts providing the required data would be helpful in studying these phenomena. Statistical data may be difficult to obtain, and some of the information may be provided in a supporting table, but it would still be useful to provide a separate flow in the standard accounts for this type of private consumption.

Goods and services may in some instances be purchased by one sector but actually consumed by another. The SNA general principle in such cases is that the consumption should be charged to the sector which makes the purchase of the final goods or services.

In the opening words to the analysis of indirect taxes and the subsidies flows it was hinted that all consumption expenditures, including those of households as well as governments, are estimated at market prices.

General government consumption expenditure (C_p), is the second flow on the credit side of account 1.

Compensation of government employees and pay and allowances to armed forces usually constitute the major part of this flow. Also included are the purchases of goods and services by government from enterprises and from the rest of the world less purchases by enterprises and households from general government. The purchases of goods and services from general government must not be confused with the purchases from government enterprises. The goods and services purchased from general government consist mainly of various small articles and services provided at museums, exhibitions, public gardens, etc.

SNA includes under government consumption expenditure all disbursements on goods – of whatever durability – for defence purposes, excluding civil defence. It should also be noted here that according to SNA, military equipment bought by the government for the use of other countries should be considered as a government consumption expenditure, and not as a transfer.

The third flow on the credit side of account 1 is *gross domestic fixed capital formation* (IF). The fixed capital in this flow consists of purchased and own account, construction work, improvement of civilian constructions, and works, and of machinery and equipment bought by enterprises and by government.

Land is defined to include inland waters and natural sub-soil deposits. The flow consists of net expenditures incurred in connexion with the acquisition of land. It also includes expenditures connected with the reclamation of land.

Under civilian construction and works are included dwellings and non-residential buildings, and other construction and works such as ways of railroads, subways, harbour facilities, airports, roads and streets, gas mains and pipes, and communication systems. The flow also includes expenditure on major alterations of dwellings and non-residential buildings and machinery and equipment. The value of the change in the work in progress on dwellings, and non-residential buildings is also included in this flow, whereas the changes in the work in progress on durable goods are included with changes in stock.

According to SNA, non-transportable fixed assets are to be included in this flow only if they are located in the territory of the country. By implication, then, all non-transportable fixed assets located outside domestic territory are not to be included in this flow. Fixed assets sent abroad or constructed and used abroad are to be entered as an investment (lending) abroad and not as a domestic capital formation.

Estimates of domestic capital formation are, as in the case of all consumption expenditures, on a market prices basis.

It would be convenient at this point to raise the problem of capital gains and losses which are not recorded in national accounts. While the accounting of realized capital gains and losses should best be left to financial transactions accounts, the unrealized capital gains and losses should, in the author's opinion, find their expression in a note to the standard national accounts. When discussing the problem of estimating the provisions for the consumption of fixed assets, attention was drawn to two commonly accepted methods, other than the replacement basis recommended by SNA, for the computation of these provisions. It was shown that by applying the straight line method, the provisions would, under increasing prices, be lower than the provisions computed on a replacement basis. The savings shown by these firms would, then, be larger than those shown by the replacement basis. The savings would however not be as large as they would be if capital gains from the increased market value of all the fixed capital of these firms were added. This can be made clear by a numerical example. The following is a simple balance sheet of a corporation after two years of operation.

Corporation X

Balance sheet as at end of second year of operation

Shares	£100 0 0	Fixed assets	£80 0 0
Profits (savings)	10 0 0	Other assets	30 0 0
	£110 0 0		£110 0 0

The original value of the fixed assets of the above corporation was £100. They were financed by shares of £100.0.0. It was estimated that the assets would serve for ten years. The allowances for depreciation were made on a straight line basis. The book value of the fixed assets as at the end of second year of operation is consequently £80.0.0.

Let us take the following simple operating account of the above corporation for the second year of its operation.

CORPORATION X

Operating account for second year of operation

Income	£20 0 0	Depreciation	£10 0 0
		Profits (saving)	10 0 0
	£20 0 0		£20 0 0

We will now assume that the market value of the corporation's fixed assets has increased during the second year of operation by 20%. Now, if the corporation were to calculate its allowances for depreciation on a replacement basis, it would have had to allow

£12.0.0. instead of the £10.0.0. allowed for on the straight line basis. This would have reduced savings from £10.0.0. to £8.0.0. However, to be consistent all the way through, the accounting records would also have to show the capital gain from the increased value of the still existing assets. They would have to show the 20% increase on the £80.0.0. being the book value of fixed assets, viz. £16.0.0. If these £16.0.0. were also shown, the savings would have amounted to £24.0.0. (£8.0.0. plus £16.0.0.) instead of £10.0.0.

Those firms which use the cumulative replacement basis method for the computation of the provisions for the consumption of fixed assets not only fail to show the capital gains on their fixed assets under increasing market prices, but also show smaller savings than would result by employing the replacement basis method. This could also be demonstrated by the example above. The allowance for depreciation on the usual replacement basis amounts to £12.0.0. But the corporation would want to make good the replacement of the fixed assets consumed during the first year. Since the allowance for the depreciation for the first year was only £10.0.0., the corporation would add another £2.0.0., which is the difference between the allowance for depreciation required as per the prices of the second year and the allowances actually made during the first year. The total depreciation on a cumulative replacement basis would thus be £14.0.0. (£12.0.0. plus £2.0.0.) This would reduce savings to only £6.0.0.

Consumers and labour organizations wishing to prove that the corporation's profits are in fact higher than shown in its accounts would perhaps agree that the allowances for depreciations should be shown as £14.0.0. They would however justly claim that the corporation has, on the other hand, also gained £16.0.0. by the increased market value. To show increased provisions for the consumption of fixed capital, i.e. to show smaller savings for a firm, and at the same time not to show the unrealized capital gains which must have been accrued to firms when provisions on a replacement basis are higher, leaves the picture of a firm's savings incomplete. It would, therefore, be highly desirable to record, in a note attached to the domestic fixed capital formation flow, the estimated figure of unrealized capital gains or losses not included in the flow.

It would also be advisable for the provisions for the consumption of fixed capital to show the different results obtained from replacement basis estimates and various other methods.

Increase in stocks (*IS*). Included in this flow are the physical changes in raw materials, work in progress and finished goods kept by enterprises. It will therefore include changes in farm stocks such as grain and livestock. It does not include the increase due to natural growth in forests and standing crops.

Changes in private gold hoardings should also be included in this flow and not as an investment in the rest of the world, as changes in monetary gold are.

SNA also recommends including in this flow changes in stocks held by the Government 'for purposes of special importance to the nation, such as building up stocks of strategic materials or emergency stocks of important commodities' [40, p. 29]. The sales of government surplus stores are deducted from this flow. If these sales were treated in a similar way to household sales, they would be deducted from government consumption. The SNA approach is then to show a larger government consumption rather than a larger increase in government stock.

It has already been pointed out that business accounting methods for recording stock movements normally differ from the replacement method. Additional differences arise from the way in which business stock is evaluated at the end of the year. These differences in fact reflect capital gains or losses. Contrary to their recommendations for fixed assets, SNA recommends in this case that wherever data for these differences are available they should be recorded in the standard accounts.

The export of goods and services (*X*) flow on the credit side of account 1 is defined on the lines of the balance of payments manual [23]. There is close collaboration between the various international organizations dealing with the compilation of international statistical data. The definitions and categories of goods and services exported and imported and of transfer payments to and from abroad have recently been co-ordinated in such a way that there are practically no differences between those employed in the manual and those of SNA. There remains of course the difference of emphasis on the categories and transactions. The balance of payments accounts can very well be regarded as one of the important supporting tables to the rest of the world account as recommended by SNA. The coverage, valuation and timing of exports and imports will be more conveniently discussed when analysing the rest of the world aceount.

Imports of goods and services (M) should technically be a debit entry. It is, however, shown on the credit side with a minus sign in order to obtain the aggregate of expenditure on gross domestic products. It has already been pointed out that this flow is defined on the lines on the balance of payments manual.

Account 2 shows the *national income aggregate* (Y), and its components. It is clearly seen from the structure of this account that national income is the counterpart of net national product at factor cost (NNP_f).

The first flow in account 2 is *compensation of employees* (YL). The major components of this flow are wages and salaries, pay and allowance of members of the armed forces, and employers' contributions to social security. The wages and salaries item is an all-inclusive item in many respects. It includes wages and salaries of residents for their services to all enterprises, to households and private non-profit institutions, to civil departments of general government and the rest of the world. It is also defined to include commissions, bonuses, tips, fees paid to directors, as well as the premium paid by employers as their participation in private pension and similar schemes not included under social security. It also includes at cost value the imputed income – income in kind – for food, lodging, and clothing when these respresent an additional benefit to employees. Lodgings or clothing which brings no additional benefit to employees are not considered as compensation. The amounts included are before the deduction of the employees' contribution to social security.

Income from *unincorporated enterprises* (*YU*) is the second component of national income. Unincorporated enterprises, as indicated before, include all sole proprietors or partners of enterprises (including farms) of all sorts and sizes as well as all independent professional men. Because of the basically individualistic character of these enterprises, labour income cannot be effectively distinguished from capital income. It is difficult to determine here whether amounts withdrawn are on account of labour or capital remuneration or reduction of capital invested. The flow therefore includes the remuneration for labour and capital whether withdrawn or retained in the business. It does not include income derived from ownership of land, buildings, and financial assets. Such income, derived from property, is shown under a separate flow where it is combined with that of households and private non-profit institutions.

In developing non-planned economies farming is usually in the form of unincorporated enterprises. Most of the other primary production is also carried out by unincorporated enterprises, or by individual households, and often not for formal trading. Some of the components of this flow are therefore of particular interest to developing countries because they involve the problem of whether and to what extent income from all primary production should be imputed. This is of interest in local economic policy and in international comparisons. The recommendations of SNA in this respect are therefore as follows:

'In the case of primary producers, that is, those engaged in agriculture, forestry, hunting, fishing, mining and quarrying, all primary production whether exchanged or not, and all other goods and services produced and exchanged are included in the total of production. In the case of other producers, that is, those engaged in all other industries listed in the *International Standard Industrial Classification*, the total of their primary production is included as for primary producers. The total of all other production exchanged by them and the unexchanged part of their production in their own trade is also included. These rules result in omitting from production the net amount of all non-primary production performed by producers outside their own trades and consumed by themselves. Non-primary production may be defined broadly as the transformation and distribution of tangible commodities as well as the rendering of services' [40, p. 5].

The initiative and entrepreneurship of a people could best be reflected by broad imputations of all its economic activities. It would therefore seem that, as Gilbert and Kravis argue, the recommendation of SNA as quoted above 'seem to be too narrow in that they would exclude considerable capital formation in under-developed countries and services rendered to Government in kind' [20, p. 66].

Income from Property (*YI*). Recorded in this flow are the actual and imputed incomes of households and private non-profit institutions from rent, interest, dividends, and corporate transfers.

The term rent as defined here includes, in addition to the actual rents received, imputed rents on owner occupied dwellings. From the sum of the actual and imputed rent are deducted all operational costs such as repairs, rates and taxes, insurance, depreciation, and mortgage interest. Included in this item also are incomes from patents, copyrights, and rights to natural resources.

Income from interest is defined here to include all actual interest received by households and private non-profit institutions in their capacity as owner of financial assets as well as imputed interest receivable from financial intermediaries.

Dividends accruing from corporations and co-operative equities held by households and private non-profit institutions are also included in this flow.

In addition to the above factor incomes, the flow includes an item which is a transfer payment – corporate transfers to households and private non-profit institutions. These consist mainly of grants, other than grants and bonuses to employees. It also includes allowances for bad debts which are also transfer payments.

The next component of national income is the *saving of corporations* (S_c). It consists of the income earned by private and public corporations and co-operatives after net payment of direct taxes and distribution of dividends. Technically it can be defined as the balance of the appropriation account of corporations. Because the incomes of private unincorporated enterprises and non-corporate public property and entrepreneurship are shown in separate flows, this flow is limited to private corporations only and does not extend to the whole enterprise sector.

Direct taxes on corporations (*TE*). Included in this flow are the taxes levied at regular intervals on corporate profits, on undistributed profits and on capital stock. Capital taxes and similar non-recurrent levies are not included in this flow. They are recorded as capital transfers from corporations to general government.

The last flow in the national income aggregate is the *general government income from property and entrepreneurship* (*YP*). In the section on *indirect taxes* (*TI*) *and subsidies* (*SU*), it was pointed out that, according to SNA, surpluses of state monopolies should be regarded as indirect taxes rather than operating profits. The covering of losses constantly sustained by Government enterprises should, on the other hand, be entered as subsidies. SNA continues by suggesting that the decision whether to record in this flow profits or losses of government enterprises is to be made after looking into the price policies pursued by the enterprises concerned and after considering whether they operate in competition with private domestic or foreign enterprises. The suggestion seems of little practical value because there are usually no competitive government enterprises.

Part of this flow is similar in character to the *income from property by households, etc., flow* (*YI*). It consists of net rent, interest, and dividends received by general government from the ownership of buildings and financial assets, all of which could be considered as factor income.

Interest on the public debt (*RP*), is not considered by SNA as a factor cost because it does not originate in production. It is a result of the method adopted for financing government consumption, and can therefore only be regarded as a transfer payment. Since these interest payments are included among some of the above income flows, they are deducted in one sum from the total income.

Interest on consumers' debt (RC) is similar in nature to interest on public debt and therefore not considered by SNA as a factor cost. It is paid to finance consumption and not production and is therefore also deducted in one sum from the income flow.

If the above two flows of interest payment are deducted from the total income flows, the national income aggregate becomes the debit total of account 2. Since national income is in fact the counterpart of net national product at factor cost, it follows that one can arrive at the latter aggregate through the various components of the national income flows.

The credit side of account 2 consists of two entries. The first is the *net domestic product at factor cost* (NDP_f) which has already been discussed. The other entry is *net factor income from the rest of the world* (YRW). Some of the value added in production in the domestic territory of an open economy may be attributable to factor services supplied by the rest of the world, while, on the other hand, residents may have provided factor services to foreign countries. The value of the factor services rendered by residents to other countries, less the value of factor services supplied from abroad, constitutes the flow of net factor income from the rest of the world. Attention should be drawn here to the fact that the term 'services' as applied in national accounts refers usually to 'non-factor services'. An example of a non-factor service is that of a professional man whose services include his factor service fee and an additional amount to cover his overhead costs. Factor services are usually referred to in national accounts as 'factor income'. By adding the flow of net factor income from the rest of the world to the net domestic product at factor cost, we arrive at the net national product at factor cost aggregate.

The debit side of account 3 is the *gross domestic capital formation* which consists of two flows discussed earlier: *gross domestic fixed capital formation* (IF) and *increase in stocks* (IS).

It is left to the credit side of account 3 to show how the gross domestic capital formation has been financed. The first flow on the credit side of this account is the *saving of corporations* (S_c) discussed in connexion with account 2. The second item – *provisions for fixed capital consumption in corporations* – is the corporations' part of the total of these provisions already discussed.

Net capital transfers to corporation (TRC), is the third flow towards the financing of capital formation. It is on the lines of the basic concepts discussed earlier, that SNA defines capital transfers as unilateral transfers considered to contribute to the financing of capital formation. Capital transfers from corporations mainly consist of grants to foundations (part of the households, etc. sector), capital levies raised by government and confiscations. The flow in the opposite direction consists mainly of war damage payments and investments grants of government to corporations. It also includes provisions made by the government for the financing of net capital formation by government enterprise. All transfers from corporations to the rest of the world and transfers from the rest of the world to corporations are assumed to be of a capital nature.

Net borrowing of corporations (L). An exceptional feature of SNA is the recommendation to include a lending and borrowing flow for each of the domestic sectors as well as for rest of the world. This is in our opinion a serious shortcoming of SNA. The system has not been designed to show domestic intrasectorial financial transactions. This is particularly true with regard to the sectorizing of the economy. The SNA sectoring is only meaningful for final production and consumption. For these purposes an economy can be largely divided into producers (enterprises) and consumers (households). To divide financial transactions into these two broad sectors and the government means including various transactors whose financial activities are far from being similar. This produces a wrong impression of the financial interests of the various segments of the economy and their share in financial transactions.

Intra domestic lendings and borrowings cancel out and consequently do not add to the total domestic capital formation. Introducing lending flow for each domestic sector therefore forms a link between the *financial transactions* of various transactors in an economy. To include a financial aspect into a system which is generally not designed for it could be more misleading than helpful.

It will be noted that account 3 provides a domestic capital formation aggregate. To arrive at a national capital formation, the net lending to the rest of the world has to be added. The latter flow appears on the credit side of the account, i.e. as a net borrowing from the rest of the world.

The last two flows of the credit side of account 3 will be more conveniently discussed in connexion with accounts 4 and 5.

In terms of the basic accounts, the current account of account 4 can be regarded as a combination of the production and appropriation accounts of the households, etc. sector. The first three flows on the debit side of the current account have already been examined. The last two flows – *current transfers* (TR) – are self-explanatory in the light of the basic concepts discussed.

The only two items on the debit side requiring some brief notes are direct taxes, and saving.

Direct taxes (T). Included in this flow are the social security contributions of employers and employees. It mainly includes, as its name implies, taxes imposed upon the incomes of households and private non-profit institutions.

Saving (S_h) is the positive or negative (dissaving) balance in the appropriate account. Differently put, it is the surplus (or deficit) of the current receipts over the current disbursements of the households sector. If positive it is part of the funds which serve to finance capital formation; if negative – it shows to what extent this sector drew from other sectors to defray its current expenditure.

The *capital reconciliation account* of account 4 records on its credit side all capital receipts such as provisions for fixed capital consumption of households, net capital transfers and net borrowing. These receipts plus the saving item transferred from the current account of the sector constitute the sector's participation in the financing of gross domestic capital formation.

The only item on the debit side of this part of the account – *finance of gross capital formation in non-corporate private sector* (F_h), is identical with the total of the capital sources. It appears as a credit flow in account 3 indicating the contribution of the households, etc. sector to the financing of domestic capital formation.

Most of the flows in account 5 of general government have been discussed earlier. The transfers to households include all social security payments by Government to the unemployed, old age pensioners, etc. Government contribution to private education and research, grants to private hospitals and sickness benefits are also included in this flow. Subsidies to the households sector such as the value of coupons issued to the population to enable them to buy at prices lower than the market prices are also included in Government transfers to households. All transfers by general government to enterprises are regarded as subsidies and recorded as such.

Transfers to and from the rest of the world include all grants in cash and kind – except military equipment which is charged to government consumption.

Saving (S_p) is the excess of all general government current revenues over current disbursements. The name saving can only be justified on the grounds that it is a forced saving on the part of households and/or enterprises.

Account 6, which is the account of the rest of the world, contains the same flows, except one – surplus of nation on current account, which appeared in the previous accounts. *The surplus of nation* (SN) is, broadly speaking, analogous to the saving flows of the domestic sectors. It is the surplus (or deficit from the point of view of rest of the world) of exports, net factor income and net current transfers from rest of the world over imports. It would be of interest to point out here in broad lines the coverage, valuation, and timing of the export and import flows.

Exports and imports cover all international changes of ownership of goods that at some stage cross the customs frontier of the domestic territory. In addition to this, which is usually the largest volume of goods, it also includes (1) goods exported or imported for storage and processing, (2) goods exported or imported for rental, (3) all marine products caught and sold abroad, (4) purchases and sales of ships and other carriers, (5) goods purchased in one foreign country by a government for its own use in another foreign country, and (6) all non-factor services.

The preferable valuation basis is f.o.b. the customs frontier of the exporting country for both exports and imports. Such a valuation basis makes the export and import of goods data comparable as between trading countries. There are however countries who cannot for some reason compile the data of imports on an f.o.b. basis and consequently value their imports on a c.i.f. basis.

Since the coverage of exports and imports refers to changes in ownership it also follows that the exports and imports should be recorded for the time at which ownership changes. Estimates are however often difficult to obtain on this type of timing. Readily available data is only to be found when the goods have crossed the customs boundaries.

Though account 6 is based on the data available for the construction of the balance of payments accounts, the emphasis on the two accounts is different. In the balance of payments accounts the major emphasis is on the detailed classification of transactions in goods and services by type, whereas the emphasis in the rest of the world account is on the aggregate of goods and non-factor services, factor income, and current or capital transfers.

C. EXPLICIT AND DERIVED AGGREGATES

A great deal of essential information for public policy-making and for decision-making by other bodies can be derived from the national accounts as they stand. One can see at first glance what was the country's gross product during the year under report, or what part of the gross product has been consumed by the government, or to what extent the country was dependent on imports from abroad. One can readily see what share of the national income went to employees as compensation for their work and what part was left with the corporations in the form of savings ploughed back into the business. One can also easily see what part of the household's income was consumed by the household, or how much of the government's revenue was in the form of indirect taxes. There are however some combinations of flows which cannot be observed at a first reading of the account. They can, however, be derived without much difficulty.

SNA, as we have seen, explicitly provides the following major aggregates; national income (Y) and its counterpart – net national product at factor cost (NNP$_f$), gross domestic product at market price (GDP$_m$), and gross domestic capital formation, (GI). Some other important aggregates widely used in economic analysis can, as shown below, be easily derived. The aggregates will of course be based upon the flows as given and defined by SNA. For this purpose the same symbols will be used as were given to each of the flows and aggregates mentioned in the foregoing pages. Three more symbols should be added here: D$_e$ – Provisions for fixed capital consumption in corporations; D$_h$ – Provisions for fixed capital consumption in households, etc., D$_p$ – Provisions for fixed capital consumption in general government. The sum of these three flows is equal to D.

Since current transfers (TR), capital transfers (TRC), and lending or borrowing (L) can flow from one domestic sector to another, and between the rest of the world and each of the domestic sectors, it is desirable to have some additional indication as to the direction of the flow. The domestic sectors and the rest of the world will therefore be numbered as follows: enterprises = 1; households = 2; general government = 3; rest of the world = 4. Using these numbers as subscripts to the above symbols, a current transfer from, say, the general government sector to the households sector will be denoted as TR$_{32}$; and a capital transfer from the rest of the world to general government as TRC$_{43}$. Lending by enterprises to households will be denoted by L$_{12}$, while borrowing by general government from households will be marked L$_{23}$.

1. Net domestic product at factor cost = NDP$_f$ $\equiv$ C$_h$+C$_p$+ IF+IS+X−M−D−TI+SU.

2. Gross domestic product at factor cost = GDP$_f$ $\equiv$ NDP$_f$+D $\equiv$ C$_h$+C$_p$+IF+IS+X−M−TI+SU.

F

3. Gross domestic product at market prices $= GDP_m \equiv GDP_f + TI + SU \equiv C_h + C_p + IF + IS + X - M.$

4. Net national product at factor cost $=$ $NNP_f \equiv NDP_f + YRW \equiv C_h + C_p + IF + IS - D - TI + SU + X - M + YRW.$

   From the current part of Account 6, we know that:
   $$X + YRW + (TR_{42} + TR_{43}) \equiv M + (TR_{24} + TR_{34}) + SN$$
   or $X - M + YRW \equiv SN + (TR_{24} + TR_{34}) - (TR_{42} + TR_{43})$
   Hence $NNP_f \equiv C_h + C_p + IF + IS - D - TI + SU + SN + (TR_{24} + TR_{34}) - (TR_{42} + TR_{43})$

5. National income $= Y \equiv YL + YU + YI + S_e + TE + YP - RP - RC \equiv NNP \equiv C_h + C_p + IF + IS - D - TI + SU + SN + (TR_{24} + TR_{34}) - (TR_{42} + TR_{43})$

6. Net national product at market prices $= NNP_m \equiv NNP_f + TI - SU \equiv C_h + C_p + IF + IS - D + SN + (TR_{24} + TR_{34}) - (TR_{42} + TR_{43})$

7. Gross national product at factor cost $= GNP_f \equiv NNP_f + D \equiv YL + YU + YI + S_e + TE + YP - RP - RC + D$

8. Gross national product at market prices $= GNP_m \equiv GNP_f + TI - SU \equiv Y + D + TI - SU \equiv GDP_m + YRW$

9. Gross domestic capital formation $= GI \equiv IF + IS \equiv S_e + D_e + (TRC_{21} + TRC_{31} + TRC_{41}) - (TRC_{12} + TRC_{13} + TRC_{14}) + (L_{21} + L_{31} + L_{41}) - (L_{12} + L_{13} + L_{14}) + F_h + F_p$

   From the capital reconciliation account of account 4 we have:
   $F_h \equiv S_h + D_h + (TRC_{12} - TRC_{21}) + (TRC_{32} - TRC_{23}) + (TRC_{42} - TRC_{24}) + (L_{12} + L_{32} + L_{42}) - (L_{21} + L_{23} + L_{24}) \equiv S_h + D_h + (TRC_{12} + TRC_{32} + TRC_{42}) - (TRC_{21} + TRC_{23} + TRC_{24}) + (L_{12} + L_{32} + L_{42}) - (L_{21} + L_{23} + L_{24})$

   From the capital reconciliation account of account 5 we have:
   $F_p + (TRC_{31} - TRC_{13}) + (TRC_{32} - TRC_{23}) \equiv S_p + D_p + (TRC_{43} - TRC_{34}) + (L_{13} + L_{23} + L_{43}) - (L_{31} + L_{32} + L_{34})$
   $F_p \equiv S_p + D_p + (TRC_{13} + TRC_{23} + TRC_{43}) - (TRC_{31} + TRC_{32} + TRC_{34}) + (L_{13} + L_{23} + L_{43}) - (L_{31} + L_{32} + L_{34})$

Hence $GI \equiv S_e + D_e + (TRC_{21} + TRC_{31} + TRC_{41}) - (TRC_{12} + TRC_{13} + TRC_{14}) + (L_{21} + L_{31} + L_{41}) - (L_{12} + L_{13} + L_{14}) + S_h + D_h + (TRC_{12} + TRC_{32} + TRC_{42}) - (TRC_{21} + TRC_{23} + TRC_{24}) + (L_{12} + L_{32} + L_{42}) - (L_{21} + L_{23} + L_{24}) + S_p + D_p + (TRC_{13} + TRC_{23} + TRC_{43}) - (TRC_{31} + TRC_{32} + TRC_{34}) + (L_{13} + L_{23} + L_{43}) - (L_{31} + L_{32} + L_{34}) \equiv S_e + S_p + S_h + D + (TRC_{41} + TRC_{42} + TRC_{43}) - (TRC_{14} + TRC_{24} + TRC_{34}) + (L_{41} + L_{42} + L_{43}) - (L_{14} + L_{24} + L_{34})$

10. Gross national investment – GNI $\equiv GI + (L_{14} + L_{24} + L_{34}) - (L_{41} + L_{42} + L_{43}) \equiv S_e + S_h + S_p + D + (TRC_{41} + TRC_{42} + TRC_{43}) - (TRC_{14} + TRC_{24} + TRC_{34})$

11. Net domestic capital formation = NI $\equiv GI - D$

12. Personal income = YH $\equiv YL + YU + YI - RC + TR_{32} + TR_{42}$

13. Disposable income of persons = YHD $\equiv YH - T - TR_{23} - TR_{24} \equiv C_h + S_h$

D. FINANCING FINAL PRODUCTS – BY SECTOR AND BY NATION

The constant flow of cash receipts and payments, and the various 'book transactions' expressed in money terms which we witness in a market economy constitute a complicated network of flows.

Households etc., finance their consumption and participation in the capital formation of the nation mainly by the compensation they obtain for rendering factor services to the productive activities of the society. Two other financing sources are the net current and capital transfers and net loans they receive from other sectors and the rest of the world.

Out of current receipts, i.e.: income from factor services, net of interest on consumers debt, and current transfers which together form their personal income (YH), households etc. make current transfers to the other sectors and also pay direct taxes to general government. The balance which remains after these payments by households etc. are made, is the disposable incomes of Households

(YHD). If households etc. do not use up all their disposable income through consumption, a saving balance is left which, together with the provisions for fixed capital consumption in households, and/or net capital transfers received from the other sectors and the rest of the world, is used for lending to other sectors and the rest of the world and for financing gross domestic capital formation. If consumption exceeds the disposable income, there is a dissaving balance in the sector which is covered by capital transfers and borrowing from other sectors and the rest of the world.

In discussing derived aggregates earlier in the book it was shown how the disposable income of households can be derived from the flows given in the accounts. The disposable income aggregate is of great interest to labour organizations and to businessmen in the trading industries. The amount that households have at their disposal for consumption or saving, rather than their total current income before taxes and other transfers, is of primary importance to such bodies.

The largest sources for the current receipts of general government are direct and indirect taxes and current transfers from other sectors. The income from productive activity constitutes a minor part of these sources. The balance left after deducting from the revenues and productive income all the current transfers and subsidies general government makes to the other sectors is at the disposal of general government for consumption expenditures. The saving balance, (S_p), less the net capital transfers made to other sectors and the rest of the world, and less provisions for fixed capital consumption in government, serve to finance the gross national investment. Dissaving is financed by capital transfers received and/or loans obtained from other sectors and/or from the rest of the world.

The operating profits of corporations (S_c) and their share in the provisions for fixed capital consumption in corporations are used to finance gross national investments. The net capital formation within the sector may exceed the savings of corporations, because they may have received capital transfers from other sectors and the rest of the world, and/or may have drawn upon other sectors by borrowing from them. Net losses incurred by corporations are also financed by capital transfers and/or borrowings from the other sectors and/or the rest of the world.

Four sources are available for financing domestic capital formation. They are: (1) The savings of private and public corporations, of households etc., and of general government; (2) the provisions made for the consumption of the fixed capital in production; (3) net capital transfers from the rest of the world, also known as international transfers; and (4) net borrowings from abroad. These last two sources are used to cover the deficit of the nation on current account, that is to say, the excess of imports plus factor income and current transfers paid abroad, over the exports plus factor incomes and current transfers received from the rest of the world. Alternatively, of course, and more happily, the first two sources may not only cover domestic capital formation but also serve for capital transfers and loans abroad.

E. SOME GROUNDS FOR CRITICISM

A great part of the discussion of SNA was of a mainly descriptive character because the system is used as a standard for comparison with other systems of national accounts discussed later in this section. It is also relevant to the discussion of the input output system which is closely linked with the domestic product and income accounts of the national accounts. While the discussion of SNA showed its many positive aspects as a social accounting system, several shortcomings were also observed. The following are some major criticisms

1. The recording of borrowings between domestic sectors introduces a financial element which is altogether alien to a system designed for the economic transactions of a nation. Neither the sectoring nor the accounting structure were designed for financial transactions. The conceptual differences in the approach to the structure of national accounts, as compared with the approach to financial transactions accounts, cannot be overstressed.

2. SNA limits imputed incomes only to those incomes which are in fact derived from activities which have an unambiguous market value. This is a limited scope for a system which is oriented to measure the welfare of a society. All the activities of any group which may be considered part of the nation's labour resources must be imputed in the nation's income. A distinction should be made between activities which are of an economic character and those which are of a recreational character. No difference should be made between 'market' and 'non-market' activities. It was also indicated which imputed activities should be charged to consumption and which to capital formation. SNA, which aims at the comparison of final product and income in developed and developing countries, whether their economies are planned or not, should have a wider definition of imputations.

3. The households sector as defined now is too all-inclusive to be of use in the analysis of market trends and of the welfare of a society. It would therefore be desirable to divide the households sector into wage earners and others.

4. The transactions of public enterprises, i.e. government enterprises and public corporations, should be separated from those of the enterprise sector. The aims and method of operation of public enterprises differ from those of private enterprises. Their profits cannot easily be distinguished from indirect taxes, while their losses can also be regarded as subsidies to their clients.

5. The consumption of durable goods should be separately indicated in the standard accounts. The separation of durable goods from other consumer goods would be of interest in the analysis of the level of welfare of a country and would be of particular importance in the analysis of consumption in developing countries where expenditures on durable goods cannot be regarded as ordinary consumption expenditures.

II · THE ORGANIZATION FOR EUROPEAN ECONOMIC CO-OPERATION STANDARDIZED SYSTEM OF NATIONAL ACCOUNTS

In so far as the basic concepts and definitions of the various flows are concerned, there are at present practically no differences between the SNA and the OEEC system [28]. There are also no differences in the basic structure of the accounts and in the sectoring of the economy. This uniformity is undoubtedly due to the very close collaboration between the statistical commission of the united nations and the national accounts experts of the OEEC (now OECD).

But while the concepts, definitions, and basic accounts are virtually identical, the structure of the national accounts, or standard accounts in SNA terminology, differs in many respects from that of the SNA standard accounts and their components.

There are six national accounts in the OEEC system. They are: Account 1 – National product and expenditure, Account 2 – National income account; Account 3 – Consolidated appropriation account for general government: Account 4 – Consolidated appropriation account for households and private non-profit institutions; Account 5 – Consolidated capital transaction account; Account 6 – Consolidated account for the rest of the world.

Using the symbols for the flows given earlier for SNA, the following matrix would represent the above six accounts. The numbers of the headings refer to the numbers of the accounts as listed above.

Account 1 of the OEEC system provides the GNP_m – an aggregate which in SNA can only be derived from the other given flows and aggregates. The approach to the construction of this account is also different from that of SNA. It may be recalled that the first item in Account 1 of SNA is net domestic product at factor cost (NDP_f).

OEEC, on the other hand, opens its national product and expenditure account with the national income aggregate which is identical with NNP_f. There are consequently in the OEEC system no direct estimates of the gross domestic product at market price – GDP_m.

OEEC Standardized System of National Accounts in Matrix Form

Credit / Debit	1	2	3	4	5	6
1			C_p	C_h	GI	X^1 $-M^1$
2	Y					
3	TI $-SU$	TE YP $-RP$		T		TR
4		YL $(YU+YI)$ $-RC$	TR			TR
5	D	S_e	S_p	S_h		TRC
6			TR	TR	L	

It was seen that SNA recommends separate flows for the export and import of goods and non-factor services, and a separate net flow of factor incomes from abroad. In the OEEC national accounts there is no separate flow for net factor income from abroad (YRW). The export flow (X^1) is combined with the factor income received from abroad, while the import flow (M^1) includes the factor income paid to the rest of the world. In view of the fact that the components of factor income from abroad are in some European countries becoming increasingly important in weight, it would seem desirable to have this component recorded as a separate flow. It is particularly important to labour organizations to have separate data about the foreign labour employed in the country or local labour employed in foreign countries, and their respective incomes. To the financial world the incomes from or payments to foreign countries on account of interest and dividends are also of special interest. A separation of the exports and imports into goods and non-factor services on the one hand, and factor services on the other is therefore highly desirable. Such a breakdown of the export and import aggregates is also to be recommended in SNA where YRW is a net flow.

The debit side of account 2 is similar to that of SNA except for the fact that OEEC combines in one flow the income from unincorporated enterprises and the income from property of households etc.

A major difference between SNA and OEEC national accounts lies in the fact that OEEC national accounts do not have capital reconciliation accounts – neither for the household etc., and general government sectors, nor for the rest of the world. This means among other things, that OEEC, unlike SNA, does not present in its national accounts the capital transfers and loans between domestic sectors. It will become apparent from further comparisons of national accounts that the SNA method of showing current and capital accounts separately for the households and government sectors and for the rest of the world has not been adopted by the industrially developed countries. They practically all follow the OEEC method in this respect. While it would not appear useful for national accounts to show loans between sectors, it would seem desirable to distinguish current transfers from capital transfers because of their different impact on the economy and the better estimates of savings and investments which result from such distinction. It should be noted here in anticipation of the discussion of the UK system of national accounts that though the UK system does not have separate current and capital accounts as recommended by SNA, it does record some of the capital transfers separately. Because of this difference, account 3 is similar only to the current account part of SNA account 5. It should be noted that the current transfers to households etc. are shown net, i.e. current transfers from general government to households etc. less the current transfers in the opposite flow.

Interest on consumers' debt flow in OEEC account 4 is treated differently than in its SNA counterpart – the current account part of account 4. In the OEEC account 4 it appears as a deduction from the income from property and entrepreneurship while in SNA it is shown on the debit side i.e. as another expenditure of households etc. SNA thereby shows the gross current income of households etc. and how it has been disposed of. The OEEC system is technically consistent in this respect, since the interest on public debt in the government account is also deducted from Government income from property and entrepreneurship. However the advantage of showing the gross income of households etc. is more important than technical consistency.

The OEEC system, unlike SNA, does not show any intersectoral loans and borrowings, but only net loans abroad.

Direct tax flow is defined slightly differently in this account from the SNA definition. OEEC recommends the inclusion of fines and penalties into this flow, while SNA includes these compulsory payments in other current transfers to general government. The SNA definition seems preferable. Direct tax flow should be limited to taxes which are directly connected with and proportional to the income of households.

OEEC account 5, which shows gross national capital formation, includes the net capital transfers and lending movement between the nation and the rest of the world. The account shows gross addition to national wealth as compared with the analogous account 3 of SNA which shows only gross domestic capital formation. While OEEC presents the net lendings to the rest of the world on the debit side of the account, SNA presents this flow on the credit side of the account, directly or indirectly, as a net borrowing from the rest of the world flow. A negative net borrowing flow indicates of course net lending to the rest of the world.

SNA contains a breakdown of the provisions for fixed capital consumption in each sector while OEEC shows these provisions in one flow for all sectors.

The rest of the world in the OEEC system is a consolidated account of the current and capital flows. SNA by presenting a separate current account for the rest of the world brings out distinctly the surplus of the nation on current account – an important aggregate in the analysis of international trade.

III · UNITED KINGDOM SYSTEM OF NATIONAL INCOME AND EXPENDITURE ACCOUNTS

A. SECTORING THE ECONOMY

In the preceding two sub-sections, the discussion centered around two national accounts systems which have been drawn up mainly after the second world war by international groups of experts and for use by countries with different economic social, institutional, and organizational structures. It should therefore now be of interest to analyse a national accounts system which has been gradually developed over several decades by eminent economists and statisticians and by government statistical departments for use by a specific industrially developed economy.

The UK System divides the economy into the following three domestic sectors, two of which are further sub-divided.

a. Persons
b. Corporate enterprises:
   Companies
   Public Corporations.
c. Public Authorities:
   Central Government
   Local Authorities.

In addition to the above three sectors there is also the rest of the world sector.

The persons sector is defined similarly to the households etc., sector of SNA. There are, however, a few rather important differences. The first difference is that unincorporated enterprises, or 'self-employed individuals' in the UK terminology, are included in this sector and not in the enterprise sector. Self-employed individuals are included in the persons sector mainly because of the practical statistical difficulty of ascertaining which part of the funds withdrawn by self-employed individuals from their enterprises is on account of factor income, and which part is a withdrawal of capital, or whether the increased capital of the business is due to ploughing in undistributed profits. The UK practice of including self-employed individuals in the persons sector seems appropriate not only for the above technical reason but also because they are practically sole decision makers for their own activity and not for a group of unknown transactors. These reasons also lead in part to the fact that the enterprises sector in the UK system is limited to corporate enterprises only and not to all transactors and producers.

Another difference is that the life funds of life assurance companies are also included in the persons sector. This would seem to be mainly due to a reluctance to make the imputations required to defray the costs of the services of financial intermediaries. The author would favour leaving these funds with the life assurance companies not only because of a general attitude towards imputations which was expressed earlier, but also because the administration and aims of the life assurance companies are different from those of the personal sector. Some life policies are, incidentally, also taken out by corporations to assure the life of specially important members of staff.

Agricultural companies are 'for reasons of statistical convenience' [36, p. 143] also included in the persons sector.

The sector of corporate enterprises with its sub-division into companies and public corporations is comparable to the private and public corporations which in the SNA and OEEC systems constitute part of the enterprise sector. There is one exception of note. Government enterprises, or trading bodies in the terminology of the UK system, which in SNA are included in the enterprise sector are in the UK system included in the public authorities sector. The reasons for this are given in the following statement: 'Although the activities of these trading bodies resemble in many respects those of business enterprises, their financial integration with, and their control by, the Central Government bring them within the Central Government Sector' [36, p. 185]. As stated before, it would seem preferable to keep separate estimates of the production of government enterprises in a supporting table, but to keep this group within the enterprise sector.

With the above exception of including government trading bodies in the central government sector, the public authorities sector is defined in a manner virtually identical with that of the general government sector of SNA. The following explanation is given by the Central Statistical office for subdividing this sector; 'for some purposes a consolidation of the Central Government's transactions with those of local authorities is appropriate (for example, in analysing expenditure on education or social services); but the importance to economic activity of the policy decisions, especially of the budgetary decisions, of the Central Government justify its separation as a sector and the separate presentation of its accounts'. [36, p. 21]. Countries with state or province subdivisions would on the same grounds be justified in having a separate sector for the states or provinces. Separate data on the transactions of the central government as distinct from states or provinces or local authorities should be made available, but these should be provided in supporting tables. The main standard accounts (or summary tables in the UK terminology) should contain one consolidated account for the whole government sector.

B. THE SUMMARY TABLES

The standard accounts of the United Kingdom consist of seven 'Summary Tables'. They are: Table 1 – National income and expenditure; Table 2 – Personal income and expenditure; Table 3 – Corporate income appropriation account; Table 4 – Revenue account of central government including national insurance funds; Table 5 – Current account of local authorities; Table 6 – Combined capital account of the United Kingdom; Table 7 – Transactions with the rest of the world. It will be noted that Tables 1, 6, and 7 show the aggregate transactions of all sectors while the other four tables show the transactions of the individual sectors.

The summary Tables by themselves are not arranged on a 'from-whom-to-whom' basis. This becomes evident when one tries to put them in a matrix form. It is only with the aid of the supporting Tables that the summary Tables can be put in a matrix form. An arrangement of the summary Tables on a 'from-whom-to-whom' basis would be desirable and convenient.

Though summary Table 1 is named national income and expenditure, it shows in effect gross national product at factor cost. The capital consumption (D) is shown as a deduction in one sum from the gross national product at factor cost (GNP_f) thereby arriving at the national income aggregate. Since this deduction is made only on one side of summary Table 1, and since it is not made for the other appropriate summary tables, this deduction cannot conveniently be shown in matrix form.

The presenting of gross national product at factor cost and not at market price follows neither the procedure of SNA which gives in account 1 gross domestic product at factor cost nor that of OEEC which shows in account 1 gross national product at market price. In these international systems, indirect taxes are added and subsidies deducted from the product account, while in the UK system taxes on expenditure (indirect taxes) are deducted and subsidies added to the Expenditure Account. Since no new estimates or computational changes are involved, there seems to be no reason why the UK summary Table 1 should not in this respect follow the OEEC recommendation. The flows in the gross national product aggregate are mainly similar to those of the OEEC system in the sense that only factor income flows are shown, and these are not shown as in SNA, which links them first to the gross domestic product at factor cost as derived by industrial origin.

Rent in the product account is singled out as a separate flow. Because of the uniqueness and originality of the approach it will be of interest to quote the following statement of the central Statistical Office:

The justification for separate specifications of income derived from rent – although there is much tradition behind it – is practical rather than theoretical. The figures given which relate principally to buildings, certainly do not measure the earnings of the factor of production "land" as conceived in classical economic theory. Rent might better be regarded as a form of trading profit – the surplus on operating account derived from the business of hiring real estate – than as the earnings of a specific and distinguishable factor of production. But both the concept of rental income and the available statistics have special features which make it convenient to give separate treatment to rental income. In the first place, a large proportion of land and buildings is owned by the occupiers; hence a correspondingly large proportion of income from rent can be measured only by imputation, being estimated by reference to the market rents actually received for similar assets . . . Secondly, much of the statistical material for estimating both actual and imputed rental income is unsatisfactory; in particular, there are considerable difficulties in analysing the total income from rent between sectors of the economy. [36, p. 332].

As remarked, this is a rather original approach. The CSO regards rent as a kind of 'non-factor' service and not as a factor income.

A distribution of the gross rent (rent gross of depreciation) between the sectors is now given in the Blue Book as Table 12 [37]. Since the data is available, and because the flow is singled out in the product account it would make it convenient for the economic analyst to have the breakdown of the gross rent flow presented in the accounts of the sectors.

It should be noted here that by definition personal rent in the UK system includes only the income derived from the possession of land and buildings. This is similar to the definition in the OEEC system, but differs from SNA and also from the USA system where personal rent also includes income from patents, copyrights, and royalties for natural resources.

Income from self-employment, income of companies and corporations, income of public enterprise, and income from rent are all gross of depreciation. Data of capital consumption by type of asset and by sector are available in the Blue Book [37, Tables 60 and 61]. There seems therefore to be no reason why the above-mentioned incomes should not be shown in the summary tables net of depreciation. It would make it possible to arrive at the national income aggregate in a more meaningful and convenient manner.

The item of stock depreciation (ISA) deserves some comment. When discussing the concept of changes in stock valuation, it was pointed out that the changes in stock should in principle be on a replacement basis. The various valuation methods used in the business world have been discussed, and the statistical difficulties in adhering to the principle of measuring the real changes have been pointed out. It was also indicated later that SNA recommends showing the difference between the valuation at 'book' value and the replacement basic value. The UK system follows this procedure of showing the adjustment involved. This entry in the UK system is named 'stock appreciation'. Such an estimate is, as pointed out before, of importance in estimating capital gains and losses. The CSO, owing to its extreme care in the estimates of fixed capital consumption, should also be in a position to show the differences between the estimates of fixed capital consumption made on a replacement basis and on the methods adopted by corporate enterprise for the computation of provisions for fixed assets consumption. Such estimates would facilitate an estimate of the capital gains or losses on the increased or decreased price value of the existing fixed capital.

There is one more item in the national income and expenditure account which requires comment: the residual error (Dis). The advantage of national accounts structure over a mere compilation of economic aggregates lies in the fact that the components, flows and aggregates must not only be interrelated but also fully articulated. Such articulation not only requires but also automatically controls the consistency between the various flows and accounts. The statistical methods of estimate are not, however, such that these requirements can always be achieved, and discrepancies are liable to appear. Some of estimated flows and aggregates may be more precise and reliable than others, but it is impossible to determine with certainty which aggregate or flow is less incomplete or more accurate. The accepted method of the UK system as well as that of the US system – as will be noted later – is to have the statistical discrepancy between the total of the income flows and the total of the expenditure flows charged to the income side of production and credited to the capital formation account.

Neither SNA nor the OEEC system have separate accounts for the business enterprise or corporate sector. The USA national accounts had a 'Consolidated business income and product account', but since 1958 this account has been eliminated from the system. The lack of a special account for the enterprise sector is mainly due to the underlying general concept according to which national accounts systems are intended to show final transactions, while business enterprises are mainly engaged in intermediate transactions. The UK system, it will be noted, appreciating the need for such limitation, has adopted a procedure by which only an 'income appropriation account' for the corporate sector is shown.

The UK system differs basically from the SNA, and OEEC systems, and from the USA system, with regard to the imputation of interest income to financial intermediaries. The UK system, unlike the other systems mentioned above, does not impute additional income for financial services. It was noted that in the case of life assurance funds the UK system avoids the problem of imputation by transferring them to the persons sector. The loss on the services rendered by banks is simply disregarded. The reasons forwarded by the Central Statistical Office are expressed in the following lines:

To carry through this kind of solution would require the allocation of the charge for financial services to specific industries and sectors. There is clearly no objective basis for determining such an allocation. It is felt that a purely hypothetical distribution of these imputed charges . . . would be more misleading than the paradox of financial concerns appearing to make a steady annual loss. [36, p. 145].

Though many would agree that the development of financial institutions in a country can well serve as an indication of its general

G

economic activity, yet the problem of imputing income for financial services appears to be one of the weakest links in the whole sphere of imputation. Though one may accept the explanation that the distribution of the imputed bank charges is rather complicated and perhaps 'purely hypothetical', it would nevertheless seem that in an industrially developed country, where the services of the banking system are of vital importance and their absolute and relative value form a not insignificant part of national income, there must be some indication of the omission of this factor income. The summary tables should carry at least a note of the estimated 'loss' of the banks.

The UK system differs from SNA in the treatment of the amounts paid to public authorities in the way of fees for services which only these authorities provide, and the payment of fines and penalties. SNA recommends recording all these fees received by government and fines and penalties imposed by it as 'other transfers from households to general government.' The OEEC system recommends the inclusion of these payments among direct taxes. In the UK system all these receipts by the public authorities are included in 'taxes on expenditure'. Though insignificant from the point of view of the amounts involved, the principle involved is nevertheless important. Increases in indirect taxes are reflected by an increase in the national product and expenditure at market prices, whereas transfers do not affect these accounts.

On the expenditure side of the central government account, the treatment of government capital expenditures deserves attention. Here the UK system differs from SNA with respect to the recording of the expenditure for defence purposes. While SNA recommends the exclusion from capital formation of all expenditures on defence – except for civil defence – the UK system includes in capital formation some expenditure for military defence, such as land and buildings for married servicemen. This is justified on the grounds that these investments could also serve civil purposes. The OEEC system recommends including with Government consumption all expenditures on defence and on all equipment purchased for civil purposes.

Government expenditures on land and buildings should according to OEEC be included in its capital formation account.

As in other national accounts systems, interest payments by the public authorities are not recorded in the factor incomes but in the appropriation accounts only. The reasoning of the Central Statistical Office for considering these payments as non-factor incomes is, however, not quite similar to that of SNA, viz:

'National Debt – is regarded as a transfer payment for a different reason; namely that having arisen almost exclusively from financing abnormal current expenditures (mainly in war) it cannot, without straining language, be regarded as corresponding with any currently produced goods and services' [36, p. 2].

The abnormal character of the expenditure is stressed here and not the general principle according to which interest paid in connexion with production is a factor income, while interest paid in order to finance consumption is not.

The combined capital account of the UK system shows the gross national investments and capital transfers abroad, i.e. domestic capital formation plus net lending to foreign countries, plus capital transfers to the rest of the world. It should also be pointed out that the UK system follows the OEEC recommendation of showing only the net lending to the rest of the world. It will be recalled that SNA also shows lending flows between domestic sectors.

IV · USA SYSTEM OF INCOME AND OUTPUT ACCOUNTS

A. THE SECTORS

USA economists and statisticians, partly taking over from their English forerunners, have during the last three decades contributed a great deal to the development of methods and estimating techniques for the analysis of national income. Their work, encouraged by the public authorities and national and international organizations, has been particularly fruitful during the last decade. Government statisticians have also shown great zeal in this field. Three times during the last decade the office of business economics of the US department of commerce has introduced various changes and improvements in the US national accounts. In 1951, [52], 1954 [53] and in 1958 [54] special supplements were published describing and analyzing the concepts, methods, and sources.

As in the analysis of the UK system, it is convenient to begin with the US method of sectorizing the economy.

The domestic economy is divided into three sectors, viz: (a) the personal sector, (b) the business sector and (c) the government sector. In addition to these three domestic sectors there is the rest of the world account.

The personal sector in the US system, though similar in name to this sector in the UK system, is in fact, defined in practically the same way as the 'households and private non-profit institutions' sector of SNA. 'It consists chiefly of individuals in their capacity as income receivers and consumers, but it includes also non-profit institutions, private trust funds, and private pension, health, and welfare funds,' [53, p. 49].

The fact that the experts of the office of business economics co-operated in the work of the united nations and OEEC technical committees working towards a standard national accounting system designed to have international applicability is felt in, among other things, the definition of the business sector. The definition is absolutely identical with the SNA enterprises sector. A certain difference in the treatment of the government enterprises account will, however, later be noted.

The US system definition of the Goverment sector is similar to the SNA general government sector. Because of the rather special administrative structure of the US federal and state governments, it will be of interest to quote the definition given in [53, p. 53]. 'The government sector includes Federal and State and local General Governments and the Social Insurance funds administered by them. These funds comprise those set up under the Social Security and Railroad Retirement programmes, State health insurance funds, the retirement funds established for Government employees, and military life insurance funds.'

B. THE SUMMARY ACCOUNTS

The summary accounts, or standard accounts in SNA terminology, have undergone several important changes during the last decade. Up to 1958 the US System consisted of six summary accounts as compared with the five in use now. The previous summary accounts gave details relating to the institutional origins of production and included a separate 'Consolidated Business and Product Account'. The more significant of these details are in the present US system left to the supporting tables which contain a wealth of factual information which should be of much use in economic analysis. These supporting tables also make possible alternative presentations and interpretations of the accounts. The present summary accounts are devoted to a compact but apt presentation of the major flows and aggregates of national production and expenditure and their interrelationships.

The following five are at present in use: (1) national income and product account; (2) personal income and outlay account; (3) government receipts and expenditure account; (4) foreign transaction account; and (5) gross savings and investment account.

From the following presentation of the US summary account in a matrix form it is apparent that these accounts are fully articulated. The numbers of the columns and rows are the numbers of the accounts as enumerated above. The figures for 1960 are from [55].

Account I presents the flows of the national income and the gross national product aggregates in terms of the incomes generated in production as well as in terms of the final goods either consumed or added to capital. It is similar to a combination of the first two standard accounts of SNA.

It will be noted that on the income side of account 1, the compensation of employees flow is broken down into four parts. One part consists of the wages and salaries income of employees – private and government – before deduction of their contribution to social insurance (YL^1); the second part is 'other labour income' (YL^{11}) in which are included 'employer contributions to private

United States 'Summary Accounts' in Matrix Form
(Figures for 1960 in Billions of Dollars)

Credit / Debit	1	2	3	4	5	Totals
1		C_h 328·9	C_p 100·1	X^1 26·7 $-M^1$ $-23.·6$	GI 72·4	504·5
2	YL^1 271·3 YL^{11} 10·9 YU 48·2 YI^1 11·7 YI^{11} 18·4 YI^{111} 14·1 YI^{iv} 1·8		RP 7·8 TR 27·3 $-$TR $-9·3$			402·2
3	YL^{111} 11·5 TE 22·3 TI 45·6 (YP $-$ SU) $-0·5$	T 50·4				129·3
4			TR 1·6		L 1·5	3·1
5	S_e 8·6 YL^{iv} 0 D 43·1 ISA 0 Dis $-2·6$	S_h 22·9	S_p 1·9			73·9
Totals	504·4	402·2	129·4	3·1	73·9	

pension, health, and welfare funds; compensation for injuries; directors' fees; pay of the military reserve, and a few other minor items of labour income' [53, p. 59]; the third part is 'Employer contributions for social insurance'. The main advantage in sub-dividing this flow in the summary accounts is to show it on a complete from whom-to-whom basis. In the systems so far examined the compensation of employees, including employers' contributions to social security is transferred *in toto* to the households etc. sector, and thereafter a transfer payment of the total social security contributions – those of the employees as well as those of the employers – is made as part of the direct taxes of the household etc., sector to general government. In the US structure of the summary accounts the employers' contributions to social insurance, though also shown as part of compensation of employees, is transferred directly from the national income and product account to the government receipts and expenditure account. The fourth part of labour income – 'excess of accruals over disbursements' (YL^{1v}) though its effect was insignificant could sometimes amount to important sums. This would be particularly so when for instance negotiations for retroactive wage increases in an industry were to be concluded in favour of the employees. Remunerations of employees are estimated on the basis of the value due to them for their services rendered during the reported period. This flow emphasizes the 'receivable-payable' principle. Amounts accrued due for productive activity but not paid out are to be charged to cost of production of the period when the production took place.

The income from property (YI) flow, shown in SNA as one item, is in the US system again sub-divided. The sub-division in the US system is into four components. The first component is 'rental income of persons' (YI^1); the second – 'net interest' (YI^{11}); the third consists of 'dividends' (YI^{111}) of the corporate enterprises to the personal sector; while the fourth component is 'business transfer payments' (YI^{1v}). This last component, which in SNA terminology is named 'corporate transfer payments to households', is a relatively important expenditure in the US economy. It mainly consists of gifts from corporate bodies to the personal sector, and bad debts written off. Such a component has to be included if the sales to consumers are recorded at market price and the income of the sellers are computed net of these 'transfers'. The US System does not, however, include this component among the national income flows. It does include it among the GNP_m components. SNA, it will be recalled, recommends the inclusion of these transfers from enterprises to households as part of the households factor income from property.

The 'nontax' part of the 'indirect business tax and nontax liability' flow consists mainly of fees and penalties. This treatment of fees and penalties is similar to that of the UK system where they are included in the 'taxes on expenditure' flow. It has already been pointed out that it differs, with some justification, from the opposing recommendations of OEEC but resembles the recommendations of SNA. This flow also contains government receipts from the business sector of rent, royalties, and value of sales of products other than those sold by public corporations. When received from the personal sector, they are included with 'Personal tax and nontax payments'.

An examination of the 'current surplus of Government enterprises less subsidies' (YP-S) flow requires first an analysis of the treatment of the Government enterprises in the US system.

Though government enterprises are included in the business sector, the profits of these enterprises are not included as part of factor cost in business and instead charged against total production by having it deducted from the subsidies granted by the government to producers. This in effect resembles the method adopted by the UK system where government enterprises are included in the government sector. In the UK system trading profits of the government enterprises are included among the government's receipts out of which the expenditures including subsidies are paid. In contrast to this similarity with the UK system, the US treatment of government enterprises differs from the UK system as well as from the SNA and OEEC system with respect to the recording of capital expenditures. Fixed capital formation and changes of stock in these enterprises are charged to government consumption and not to gross domestic capital formation.

Although government enterprises are grouped in the business sector, they are treated by the US system mainly as part of the government sector, for the following reasons. Firstly, it is difficult to determine whether the profits realized are not due to special privileges enjoyed and/or to various forms of indirect aid from government departments or, conversely, whether the losses incurred might be due to general government policy being based on other than purely business considerations. Secondly, capital purchases by government are, more often than not, made in a combined deal for government and government enterprises, and the budgets provided for such expenditures are all-inclusive. Thirdly – and this is a distinct reason in favour of classifying government enterprises as part of the business sector – the current expenses of government enterprises are thereby directed to business expenses and not to final consumption. This treatment of government enterprises is probably practical for the US where these enterprises do not quantitively play an important part in the production sphere.

The combination of the current surplus of government enterprises flow with that of subsidies is also justified for the reasons mentioned and in the special circumstances of the US. The combined flow of subsidies less the current surplus of the government enterprises (to the extent that such surpluses exist) in the national income product account – where this combined flow has to be charged against the total product – appears under the name of current surplus of government enterprises less subsidies, as a negative figure. In the government receipts and expenditures account this combined flow appears on the expenditure side as subsidies less current surplus of government enterprises, but as a positive figure.

Capital consumption allowances (D) consist of allowances for the depreciation of the capital investments of the business sector, of farmers, of non-profit institutions, and of owner-occupied dwellings. The depreciation allowances for the business sector are calculated on the basis of the original cost. This is indeed an important deviation from the general principle according to which all capital consumption costs should be computed on a current replacement basis. The statistical difficulties of estimating depreciation allowances on a replacement basis are probably not the decisive factor in the US approach to this problem. It would seem that the desire to keep the provisions for fixed capital consumption in non-farm business in line with the taxation policies of the US government has more to do with it. This assumption is based on the fact that while provisions for depreciation of capital assets in all non-farm industries are on an original (historical) cost basis, the depreciation allowances for farming investments are computed on a replacement basis.

The US system shows the factor incomes net of interest received on consumers debt, and interest received on public debt. There are consequently no explicit flows in the production account showing these deductions as recommended by SNA and OEEC systems. The procedure is similar to that adopted by the UK system.

Turning now to the expenditure side of the product account, the first item is the flow of 'Personal consumption expenditure' (C_h) which is analogous to 'Private consumption expenditure' in SNA and identically defined. The personal income and outlay account gives what may be considered as a partial satisfaction to a need discussed before, the need to show the expenditure on durable goods separately, and within the framework of the standard accounts. The flow of personal consumption expenditure, in so far as it is interrelated with the production account, appears in one sum but is internally sub-divided into (a) durable goods, (b) non-durable goods and (c) services. This breakdown is of great value in economic analysis.

A similar arrangement, equally important for economic analysis, is made with regard to the gross private domestic investment (GI) which is shown structurally in the production account and in the gross saving and investment account in one combined sum. However, in the latter account the flow is internally sub-divided into: (1) new construction, (a) residential non-farm, (b) other; (2) producers durable equipment; (3) change in business inventories, (a) non-farm, (b) farm. SNA and the UK system show a structural breakdown of gross domestic capital formation into fixed capital formation and increase in stock. OEEC, on the other hand, show

(GI) in one flow. The gross saving and investment account shows the gross national investment which is similar to the method adopted in the OEEC and in the UK systems.

As the name of the flow implies, no government expenditure on capital investments are included in this flow. They are all included in the current expenditures of the government. The new construction included under the sub-flow 'other' mentioned above consists of industrial, commercial, and other non-residential buildings; construction for 'public utilities' such as railroads, telephone, and telegraph, etc. farm residential and non-residential buildings; and construction in connexion with petroleum and natural gas well-drilling.

Inventory valuation adjustment (ISA) in the US system are only in connexion with the adjusting of the non-farm inventory 'book' value to a replacement value. The farm inventory is estimated on the basis of the physical quantities of crops and livestock at the beginning and end of the reported year. The difference between these quantitites is multiplied by an average price prevailing during the year. The valuation of the changes in stock of the non-farm business is based on the book value and no adjustment is made to a replacement basis. The approach is similar to that adopted for the estimates of capital consumption allowances, as indicated above.

Export and import of goods and services include, like the OEEC system and the UK system, but unlike SNA, the factor income received from and paid to the rest of the world. The US computation of the factor income from abroad is net of taxes and also excludes the undistributed profits of subsidiaries. As to the undistributed profits of foreign subsidiaries – the UK system includes them, the OEEC system excludes them. SNA, again, recommends that undistributed profits of foreign subsidiaries which are 100% or almost 100% owned by the parent company should be included, whereas undistributed profits of subsidiaries only partly owned by a resident enterprise should be excluded.

Government purchases of goods and services (C_p) which mainly consist of the expenditures for compensation of employees and purchases of consumption good include also all capital outlay and some foreign grants. As mentioned before, all expenditure on capital investments, whether on equipment or on new construction, and whether for military purposes or for civil purposes, are included under government consumption in the US system. Moreover, all the capital investments of government enterprises are also, as indicated earlier, charged to this flow. This treatment of government capital expenditures is in striking contrast with that of the other system.

Up to 1958, when further changes were introduced in the US system [54], all international contributions were also included in this flow. The present procedure is to distinguish between foreign aid in cash and foreign aid in kind. Aid in cash is treated as a transfer payment to the rest of the world, while aid in kind continues to be recorded as part of government purchases for consumption. It will be recalled that according to SNA, all grants to foreign countries, whether in cash or in kind, should be entered as a transfer to the rest of the world. The only exception which SNA, as well as the OEEC system, recommends, is that purchases of military equipment for the use of other countries should be charged to the consumption expenditures of the granting country.

It should be mentioned that the US system does not, unlike SNA, differentiate between current and capital transfers, though these transfers contain a large percentage of transfers of an evident capital character.

Finally it is of interest to point out that the flow of 'government purchases of goods and services' (C_p) is, in the 'government receipts and expenditure account', divided into the following subflows:

Federal
    National defence (less sales)
    Other
State and local.

Two more flows in the Personal income and outlay account are divided into subflows which do not constitute part of the interlocking entries – a feature of the US system already referred to. The

flow of wage and salary disbursements (YL^1) is sub-divided into:
  (a) manufacturing,
  (b) other private,
  (c) government.

The flow of proprietors' income (YU) contains the following two subflows; (a) business and professional; (b) farm.

The negative symbol ($-TR-9.3$) which stands for 'personal contributions for social insurance' is the complementary part of the 'employer contribution for social insurance' (YL^{111}). While the latter sum is entered directly from the production account to the Government account, the former sum constitutes in the Product account an integral and non-divisible part of wages and salaries, – disbursements (YL^1) – out of which the employees' share in the contribution for social insurance is transferred from the personal account to the government account. The amount transferred is, however, not shown in the personal account as part of the personal outlay (on the debit side) but as a deduction from personal income (on the credit side). The flow of 'Personal contributions for social insurance' is indicated in the matrix by the symbol (TR), while the employers' part has been marked (YL^{111}).

V · NATIONAL INCOME AND GROSS NATIONAL PRODUCT MEASURED BY INCOME FLOWS AND EXPENDITURE FLOWS

It suffices only to look through the published reports of the international organizations concerned and of the statistical offices of some of the leading countries of the western world to realize what a tremendous amount of work has been devoted by the experts during the last decade towards reaching greater uniformity in the presentation of standard or summary accounts.

However, there still remain, as we have seen in the preceding pages, quite a number of differences which make international comparison somewhat difficult. Some of these difficulties could be overcome by referring to the supporting tables. This is particularly true in the case of the US system, where the supporting tables would be capable of satisfying any analysis, however searching and thorough. But the original intention was to express these accounts in a practical, compact, and convenient form. National accounts are the most popular of the social accounting systems. To change and improve statistical methods no doubt involves considerable expense, and requires co-operation from every sector concerned. Nevertheless, the protracted negotiations at expert conferences, even when the matter under discussion is relatively minor, leave a very bad impression. In some cases tradition, and perhaps a desire for originality, considerably impede the progress towards consistency and uniformity.

The following two tables are intended to play a double role. They are intended to show how production is measured by income and expenditure flows in the various systems. They are also intended to convey a very general view of how the production account, which is the largest of the Standard accounts, may be constructed from the existing flows in the respective standard accounts.

TABLE A

Y, GNP$_f$ and GNP$_m$ measured by Income Flows

SNA	OEEC SYSTEM	UK SYSTEM	US SYSTEM
Compensation of employees (YL)	Compensation of employees (YL)	Income from employment (YL)	Wages and salaries disbursements (YL^1)
			Other labour income (YL^{11})
			Employer contributions for social insurance (YL^{111})
			Excess of accruals over disbursements (YL^{1V})
Income from unincorporated enterprises (YU)	Income from property and entrepreneurship accruing to households, etc. (YU+YI)	Income from self-employment (YU+D)	Proprietors' income (YU)
Income from property YI		Rent (YI^1+D)	Rental income of persons (YI^{11})
			Net interest (YI^{11})
			Dividends (YI^{111})
Saving of corporations (S$_e$)	Saving of corporation (S$_e$)	Gross trading profits of companies (S$_e$+TE+D+YI^{11}+YI^{111})	Undistributed corporate profits (S$_e$)
		Gross trading surpluses of public corporations (S$_e$+TE+D+YI^{11}+YI^{111})	
		Stock appreciation (ISA)	Inventory valuationa adjustment (ISA)
Direct taxes on corporations (TE)	Direct taxes on corporations (TE)		Corporate tax liability (TE)

	Y	Y	Y	Y
General government income from property and entrepreneurship (YP)	Government income from property and entrepreneurship (YP)	Gross profits of other public enterprises (YP + D)	Capital consumption allowances (D)	
		Net income from abroad (YRW)		
Less: Interest on the public debt (RP) Interest on the consumers' debt (RC)	Less: Interest on the public debt (RP) Interest on the consumers' debt (RC)	Less: Capital consumption (D)	GNP_f	
National Income (Y)				
Provisions for domestic fixed capital consumption (D)	Depreciation and other operating provisions (D)	Capital consumption (D)	Business transfer payments (YT^{1v}) Indirect business tax and non-tax liability (TI)	
Gross National Product at factor cost GNP_f	GNP_f	GNP_f	GNP_f	
Indirect taxes (TI)	Indirect taxes (TI)	Taxes on expenditure (TI)	Current surplus of government enterprises less subsidies (YP − SU)	
Less: Subsidies (SU)	Less: Subsidies (SU)	Less: Subsidies (SU)	GNP_m	
Gross national product at market prices (GNP_m)	GNP_m	GNP_m	GNP_m	

H

TABLE B

GNP$_m$ Measured by Expenditure Flows

SNA	OEEC SYSTEM	UK SYSTEM	US SYSTEM
Private consumption expenditure (C$_h$)	Consumers' expenditure on goods and services (C$_h$)	Consumers' expenditure (C$_h$)	Personal consumption expenditure (C$_h$)
General government consumption expenditure (C$_p$)	Government current expenditure on goods and services (C$_p$)	Public authorities' current expenditure on goods and services (C$_p$)	Government purchases of goods and services (C$_p$)
Gross domestic fixed capital formation (IF)	Gross domestic asset formation (GI)	Gross fixed capital formation at home (IF)	Gross private domestic investment (GI)
Increase in stock (IS)		Value of physical increase in stock and work in progress (IS)	
Exports of goods and non-factor services (X)	Sales of goods and services to the rest of the world and factor income from the rest of the world (X^1)	Exports and income received from abroad (X^1)	Exports of goods and services (X^1)
Less: Import of goods and non-factor services (M)	*Less:* Purchases of goods and services from the rest of the world and factor income payments to the rest of the world (M^1)	*Less:* Imports and income paid abroad (M^1)	*Less:* Imports of goods and services (M^1)
Net factor income from the rest of the world (YRW)			
Gross national expenditure at market prices (GNP$_m$)	GNP$_m$	GNP$_m$	GNP$_m$

103

VI · THE FRENCH NATIONAL ACCOUNTS
(LES COMPTES DE LA NATION)

A. GENERAL CHARACTERISTICS

Though based on the same fundamental accounting structure as the other national accounts systems hitherto examined, the French system differs from the other systems in many respects. These differences, most of which could be attributed to the traditional contrasts in the presentation of quantitative economic data, have increased during the last few years. One of the principle and important innovations introduced in 1960 [16] and [17], as compared with the methods in 1956 [15], is in the field of financial transactions and balance-sheet changes. National accounts systems have limited themselves mainly to the measurement of net production, consumption, and formation of capital. The problem of integrating financial flows and changes with the national accounts system has been under serious consideration by various experts during recent years. The methods adopted by the French system will therefore be of particular interest later on when the various financial transactions systems are examined and the recommendations for the integration of social accounting systems are discussed.

B. SECTORING THE ECONOMY

The French system for sectoring the economy is unique in several respects. There are four domestic sectors, or economic agents (Agents économiques) in the French terminology. The term sector (secteur) is used for the industrial classification of enterprises. These four economic agents are:

1. Non-financial enterprises (Enterprises non-financières).
2. Households (Ménages).
3. Administration (Administrations).
4. Financial institutions (Institutions financières).

There is also a rest of the world account (compte de l'extérieur) which is sub-divided into two parts: (a) Foreign nations (Etranger) and (b) Overseas territories (Pays d'outre-mer – POM).

In the non-financial enterprises sector are included all non-financial economic units established for the production of goods and services. Consequently, this sector includes all private enterprises – whether incorporated or not, partnerships, co-operative societies, etc. farmers and professionals. It also includes all public enterprises i.e. governement enterprises and public corporations. It does not include houseowners, whether their houses are occupied by them or not, and it does not include, as the name implies, the financial intermediaries.

The household sector is generally defined as in the other national accounts systems. There are two exceptions typical to the French approach to sectoring. Firstly, private non-profit institutions are not included here, but placed in the administration sector instead. Secondly, as the system is based on domestic concepts, households include residents as well as non-residents.

The administration sector is defined as consisting of groups of people or of private or public accounting units, French or foreign, which act on a non-profit basis, and which participate in the economic life by rendering to the community and to certain individuals services of a kind which are not paid for individually. The sector contains, then, all those central and local government administrative bodies, public services, and social security institutions which constitute the general government sector of SNA. It includes, in addition, all private social security institutions and the private non-profit institutions which in SNA comprise part of the households etc. sector.

A sector which other national accounts systems do not normally have is that of financial institutions. It consists of the financial intermediaries in the economy, i.e. the banking system, non-banking credit institutions and, insurance companies. In the other systems all financial intermediaries constitute part of the enterprise sector.

C. THE TABLEAU ECONOMIQUE

Like other National Accounts systems, the French Tableau économique has the basic structure of accounts which keep the entries in the accounts interlocked. Each economic agent (sector) has in principle an operation account (compte d'exploitation), an appropriation account (compte d'affectation), and a capital account (compte de capital). The rest of the world account interrelates the external transactions of all the economic agents. The Tableau économique is in fact limited to basic accounts. There are no aggregating accounts which centralize the production, national income, or capital formation of the nation. The Tableau économique also differs from the other systems in that a number of the entries in the accounts of the French system do not follow the definition of the flows commonly known and used in economic analysis, and, consequently do not lead to the popular economic aggregates which result from the standard accounts of the other systems.

The basic accounts of each sector are first presented in the usual accounting form, the left side of which is the debit side or the 'use' (emplois) part, while the right-hand side of the account is termed 'sources' (ressources). The next step consists of presenting all these separate accounts in one combined statement. Horizontally, the entries in the various accounts remain distributed in the three basic accounts mentioned above. Vertically, the entries are classified into two categories of transactions to be discussed later. This combined statement is named in the traditional French manner 'Tableau économique'. A Tableau économique for 1960 is given in [18].

In summing up what was so far said about the accounts in the French system, we cannot do better than quote the following two sentences from [1, p. 43]:

Whereas the OEEC/UN System attempts at one and the same time to present both an accounting analysis and an instrument for the immediate derivation of economic aggregates (GNP, NI, etc.) the French system is directed primarily toward only the former objective. The tableau économique finally built up in the French system is therefore a disaggregated presentation of interrelated accounting elements.

The supporting tables of the French system of national accounts constitute in fact an expanded version of the Tableau économique.

The Services des Etudes Economiques et Financières du Ministère des Finances (SEEF) calls this double presentation of the accounts 'deux degrés de décontraction' (two stages of discontraction) [17]. The accounts of the first stage, described above in general terms, are called simplified accounts (les comptes simplifiés). The accounts of the second stage are named expanded accounts (les comptes développées). It is mainly in the expanded accounts that the financial flows and balance sheet changes mentioned are presented.

Since it is rather inconvenient, if not impossible in some cases, to derive meaningful economic aggregates directly from these accounts, the SEEF also prepares a special appendix where some of the major aggregates are given.

There are three transaction categories in the Tableau économique They are:

(1) transactions in goods and services (opérations sur biens et services),

(2) distribution transactions (opérations de répartition),

(3) financial transactions (opérations financiéres).

Because of the unique structure of the Tableau économique, only the first transaction category can be roughly compared with the gross domestic product at market prices aggregate as common in the other national accounts systems. The first flow of the first transaction category is 'Gross domestic product' (production intérieure brute). This is the equivalent of the gross domestic product at market prices aggregate. There is, however, one significant difference. The services of the administration sector are not considered in the French system as constituting production. The only two sectors which have operation accounts in the Tableau économique are the non-financial enterprises sector and the households sector. The 'sources' side of the operation accounts of these two sectors show the share of each sector in the gross domestic product.

'Consumption' (consommation), which is the second flow of the above aggregate, is defined as consisting of the final consumption by households, administration, and financial institutions as shown on the 'uses' side of the appropriation accounts of these sectors. The consumption of households includes goods of any durability, and goods produced for own use. The consumption of administration is defined in a manner similar to that of general government consumption in SNA. The consumption of the financial institutions is on a net basis. It consists of the difference between the price of the small services rendered by the institutions less the expenses for goods and services. The French system, similar to the UK system, does not impute any additional service costs.

'Gross fixed capital formation'. (Formation brute de capital fixe) practically follows the SNA definition.

'Increase in stock' (formation de stocks et divers), is also defined like SNA. The valuation, however, is different. It is based on the difference between the stock at the beginning of the year and that at the end of the year multiplied at an average price. The valuation method, then, is similar, except for the farm product, to the method used in the USA accounts.

Domestic Product

	£		£
Gross domestic product at market price	251,030	Consumption of household	175,720
		Consumption of administration	12,540
		Consumption of financial institutions	1,280
		Fixed capital formation	49,670
		Increase in stock	5,120
		Exports (including net non-factor services)	37,510
		Less imports	−30,810
Gross domestic product at market prices	251,030	Expenditure on gross domestic product	251,030

Taking into account the differences in definition of the flows in this first transaction category as compared with the equivalent flows in the other national accounts systems, and recalling that the gross domestic product shown in this transaction category is at market prices, i.e. it includes the indirect taxes net of subsidies, this transaction category can be presented in the above aggregated manner. The figures are from the Tableau économique for 1960 [18]. The above domestic product account arranged on the lines of the other western national accounts can serve as an illustration of how the flows in the Tableau économique have to be manipulated in order to arrive at aggregative data which is convenient in economic analysis.

The second transaction category in the Tableau économique 'distributive transactions' (operation de répartition) – has no counterpart in the other national accounts systems. The first flow in this transaction category – salaries and social insurance (salaires et cotisations sociales) – closely resembles the compensation of employees flow in SNA. The only important difference is that it excludes the contributions of employers to private pension and similar schemes which are not included in social insurance. These payments – in cash or in kind – comprise in the French system part of the second element, viz: 'allowances and grants' (prestations sociales). The allowances and grants paid by administration consist of: (a) payments of pension paid by Administration to retired employees – civil and military, (b) family allowances, (c) reimbursement of medical treatment expenses, (d) indemnities for accidents at work.

The allowances paid by enterprises consist of two parts: (a) family allowances, (b) other grants which include also premia paid by employers to life insurance companies in favour of their employees. These allowances and grants are of the kind that the enterprises pay to their employees in addition to their obligatory social insurance contributions.

The two flows of the second transaction category analyzed above are in gross amounts. The payments made are shown in the various accounts of each sector on the 'uses' side. The incomes received are recorded on the 'sources' side.

Details of the flow of interest and dividends are given under the element of 'interest and dividends (intérêts et dividends). The interest paid by households for productive purposes is entered in the operation account, while interest paid on consumers' debt is recorded in the appropriation account.

All taxes – direct and indirect – and levies are included in the 'Taxes' (Impots) flow. The indirect taxes paid are recorded in the operation accounts, while the direct taxes are recorded in the appropriation accounts of the sectors on the 'uses' side. On the 'sources' side indirect as well as direct taxes received by the administration sector are recorded in the appropriation account of this sector. Only a technically trained statistician could find the wanted information on taxes which is important by itself and required for other aggregates. The direct taxes include those on companies and on persons. Since State monopolies are included in the enterprise sector, the excise duties levied by some of them are recorded as a receipt of the enterprise sector.

'Transfers' (transferts) is, like the previous flow, an all-inclusive element. It includes current and capital transfers from one sector to another as well as to and from abroad. It contains practically all the components of the current and capital transfers as recommended by SNA as well as the flow of subsidies from administrations to producers and households.

The 'insurance' (assurances) flow is common to both general insurance (fire, accident, and other risks) and to life insurance. The income from insurance transactions is defined in the French system as being the difference between the premia paid and indemnity received.

The 'foreign receipts and disbursements' (dépenses et recettes extérieures) flow is connected with the fact that the French system is based on purely domestic concepts. Tourists coming from abroad, or from overseas territories, temporary workers, foreign military forces, branches of foreign firms, foreign diplomatic services are all included in the respective domestic sectors as non-nationals. On the other hand French visitors abroad, Frenchmen working temporarily abroad, or serving in the military forces abroad are considered as external nationals. The amounts received from abroad to cover the expenses of the non-national residents are credited (sources) to the respective sectors and charged to the external accounts. The amounts disbursed in connexion with the maintenance of the external nationals are charged (uses) to the respective sectors and credited to the external accounts.

Various transfers are recorded in the 'Sundry distributive transactions' (Opérations diverses de répartition): various fines and penalties (included in SNA under 'Other transfers from households etc. to general government); revenues from licences, patents and copyrights, membership fees, and participation in the upkeep of non-profit institutions.

The 'gross income of unincorporated enterprises' (revenu brut des entrepreneurs individuels) flow contains the income, gross of depreciation allowances, of private farming, retail shops, craftsmen working on their own and independent professionals. Included in this flow are the imputed incomes from the consumption of own produced goods by farmers (autoconsommation) estimated at factor cost.

'Financing of investment by unincorporated enterprises' (Financement des investiseements par les entrepreneurs individuels) consists of that part of income which the unincorporated enterprises have not consumed in their capacity as households and which serve to increase their assets. The amount is added to the capital account of households on the 'uses' side, and as an increase in the capital account of the non-financial enterprises on the 'sources' side.

The first flow in the third transaction category is 'gross operating profits' (Résultat brut d'exploitation) which is given for the non-financial enterprises and households sectors. Only these sectors have operating accounts. It consists of the difference between the gross domestic product at market price (as defined in the French system) and the operating costs.

It has already been stated that the Tableau économique provides no economic aggregate. But even to arrive at a single aggregate one has to combine figures from different accounts from both sides (uses and sources) of the Tableau. This could be observed from the discussion of the last flows. The derivation of the gross saving is another illustration. The gross saving (épargne brute) of a sector is the balance of its appropriation account, i.e. the gross operating profits (for the non-financial enterprises and household sectors which have operation accounts) plus the totals of transactions in goods and services and of distribution transactions of the 'sources' side of the appropriation account, minus the totals of transactions in goods and services and of distribution transactions of the 'uses' side of the appropriation account. Details of the composition of flows in the financial operations category are given in the expanded accounts of the system. In these accounts the French system combines the accounting of the production and consumption activities of an economy with that of its financial transactions. The expanded accounts will be examined in a later chapter.

VII · USSR CONCEPTS OF NATIONAL INCOME (NATSIONAL'NY DOKHOD)

A. PRODUCTION AND INCOME

A planned economy must by its very nature rely a great deal on the accounting and statistical data of the various units of economic activity. Indeed it is known that comparatively large staffs in the USSR are occupied in the compiling and preparing of the abundant statistical and accounting data. The concepts and methods applied in the USSR are known to the outside world mainly from dispersed quasi-official methodological writings in this sphere. Though the available methodological studies on the concepts of the USSR national income accounts may not fully or exactly describe the concepts adopted in practice by the central statistical board of the USSR, it may, however, be presumed that they are very close to those actually employed in the USSR. The studies were written by well-known USSR statisticians of national income.

Income, according to USSR concepts, originates from and is equal to production. There is of course nothing different in this concept from that adopted in western national accounts. The difference however lies in the definition of production, or more precisely 'social production'. But first let us examine the USSR concept of the 'social product'. These are defined as 'the aggregate of consumable material goods produced in the branches of national production' [61, p. 78]. The word 'consumable' in the above definition is of importance because it implies that the goods produced must be of a type that can be consumed – currently or within a certain period of years. The social product must also be made in the branches of material production which implies that work done outside these branches, such as housework etc., is not considered a social product. The material form of the product is somewhat broadly defined in the sense that it is not limited to physical goods. It also includes for instance the energy produced from natural resources.

Social production according to USSR concepts consists of the provision of social products by social labour engaged in the branches of material production. This definition differs in several respects from that of the western world. The two major differences in the USSR concept of social production are as follows:

(1) It is limited to social products (material products mainly), while according to the western definition production embraces all goods and services satisfying human wants measurable in monetary terms.

(2) It is related to one factor only, viz: social labour, whereas according to western economic concepts the factors of production consist, in addition to labour, also of land, capital, and entrepreneurship.

The following is a list of services which are excluded from social production as listed in [42].

(a) Material and communal services which cover passenger transportation, a large part of communication, public baths, laundries, housing, recreation and entertainment, sanitation services, barber shops etc.

(b) Other services to individuals – those of teachers, physicians, nurses, etc.

(c) Administration and defence.

(d) Science and research.

(e) Banks and insurance.

Social products are in Soviet theory divided into two main categories: category 'A' and category 'B'.

Category 'A' includes all intermediate goods required for social production, and productive accumulation which consists of the increase in physical stock and fixed assets required in connexion with social production.

Category 'B' consists of goods leaving production, and of non-productive accumulation. The goods leaving production are current and durable goods – except dwellings – consumed by the population, while the non-productive accumulation consists of dwellings, schools, hospitals etc., which have been constructed for rendering services in the future.

Gross social product as conceived in the USSR accounts consists not only of the final social products but also of the material input (intermediate products) in production. The USSR concept of gross product is double gross: firstly because allowance for consumption of fixed capital is not deducted; and secondly, because intermediate goods are not excluded. The USSR concept of gross product is based on the Marxian concept according to which the value of social product consists of two components: (1) The reproduced or 'transferred value'. This component, which has been denoted by the letter 'c', shows the value of producers durables and materials consumed in the course of production; (2) The value added component which is sub-divided into two parts: (a) sum of wages paid denoted by the letter 'v', and (b) realized profits denoted by the letter 'm'.

The net social product which is equal to the gross social product less the material input (c) is similar to the net national product at factor cost in the western national accounts systems. The major difference is that the USSR aggregate does not include 'services'.

Soviet economists in [24 and 25], and in [63, p. 154] have been trying to prove that the 'services' (double counting) included in the NNP_f of the US national accounts amount to 20–30% of the GNP_m. Soviet authorities would however not agree that, conversely, to arrive at a national product of the Soviet economy according to western concepts, the same percentage should be added to Soviet figures of net product. The following excerpts from [43, p. 3] give some indication as to why The Central Statistical Board of the USSR object to such calculations: 'Since there is a difference in the relative weight of services in the USSR and other countries, this 'double counting' would affect the values obtained to a different degree; consequently, the relationships for individual countries could not provide a basis for a true comparison between the product and national income estimates of different countries'.

In the Soviet national income aggregate the net social product is composed of the primary income of the population and that of the enterprises in the productive sphere.

The primary income of the population is that part of income which is derived by the social labour force, i.e. labour producing 'social products' as explained above. It includes the income of individual artisans and farmers, who in SNA are part of the unincorporated private enterprises.

Primary income of enterprises in the productive sphere is divided into two parts: one part of the income accrues to the State and consists of 'turnover taxes', a part of the profits, contributions to social insurance, minor taxes and other levies on enterprises, and interest on short term credit; the other part accrues to the enterprises and consists of the balance of profits and contributions to certain funds. The profits left with the enterprises are subject to and are given as an incentive for plan fulfilment. The contributions to funds are for the acquisition of fixed assets and increase in working capital.

B. THE SECTORS

Soviet economy is divided for the purpose of national income accounts into the following three basic sectors:

(a) Socialist productive enterprises,
(b) non-productive sphere, and
(c) the population

Branches of material production and type of ownership	Gross product	Materials consumed in production	Net product
1. Industry			
(a) State enterprises			
(b) Co-operative – Kolkhoz enterprises			
2. Construction			
(a) State enterprises			
(b) Co-operative Kolkhoz enterprises			
(c) Private dwelling houses of the population			
3. Agriculture			
(a) State enterprises (sovkhoz, machinery and tractor stations – M.T.S.)			
(b) Kolkhozi			
(c) Auxiliary farms of kolkhozniki			
(d) Auxiliary farms of workers and employees			
(e) Private farms of farmers individualists			
4. Forestry			
5. Transportation and communication			
(a) State enterprises			
(b) Co-operative kolkhoz enterprises			
6. Supply and storage			
7. Trade and catering (wholesale and retail)			
(a) State enterprises			
(b) Co-operative kolkhoz enterprises			
8. Procurement of farm products			
9. Miscellaneous			
Total			

The socialist productive enterprises sector can best be described by the branches of social production of which it is composed. The above table shows a classification of these branches and the type of ownership as presented in (2, p. 24] where it is used to indicate a scheme for the computation of national income.

The non-productive sphere sector consists, in broad lines, of the following:

(1) Government departments of defence, health and education,

(2) The post-office and similar organizations which though included in the State financial budget are usually self-supporting.

(3) Enterprises which either independently or in association with productive enterprises provide services on a commercial basis,

(4) Organizations which provide services against membership fees and dues.

The population sector consists of all persons living in individual or institutional households, in their capacity as consumers, whether employed in productive or non-productive activities.

C. MARKETS, PRICES, AND NATIONAL INCOME FIGURES

In the structure of the Soviet market and the determination of prices lies probably the major differences between planned and non-planned economies. The incomparability of the USSR national income accounts with those of the west is largely due to the problem of determining prices and evaluating production. The determination of price in a 'free' market is altogether different from that in the 'markets' of planned economies.

There are at present three markets in the Soviet economy:

(a) the internal market,

(b) the organized consumer goods market, and

(c) the non-organized or collective farm market.

The internal market is where the producers' materials, construction and equipment, are traded within the productive sector. Since these transactions are centrally planned, the prices for the products of each industry are fixed in a way that they should suffice to defray the cost of labour, materials and depreciation – 'present' and 'past' labour – plus a small average profit. Two points should be parenthetically mentioned here:

(a) the input of materials is valued at the cost of labour required for the replacement of these materials;

(b) the consumption of fixed assets (which together with material input are termed in Soviet theory 'productive consumption') is also evaluated at the cost of labour required to replace the assets.

This is similar to the SNA principle of evaluating at replacement value all increase in stock and consumption of fixed assets. Similar to SNA recommendations the Soviet practice is also to include foreseen obsolesence in depreciation costs.

In the organized consumer goods market, where consumer goods are sold by the State and the co-operative retail trade, prices are also fixed by plan, but on a different basis. In addition to the cost of production as fixed for producers' goods, a 'turnover tax' is levied on sales.

Prices in the non-organized or 'collective farm' market for consumers are determined by laws of supply and demand, after the producers of these goods have met their obligatory deliveries to the State.

Based on the Marxian distinction between 'products' exchanged within the State sector, and 'commodities' sold by or outside that sector, Soviet economists have developed the concepts of 'value originated' and 'value realized'. According to these concepts value 'originates' in each branch of the socialist productive enterprises sector in proportion to the labour input. This value can be 'realized' by over-valuing in monetary terms consumer goods in favour of producer goods.

Because of the multiplicity of prices and because these prices are mainly fixed by central planning, it is rather difficult to make any comparison of the value of production. Western economists have argued for instance that the 'turnover taxes' and other minor taxes can be considered analogous to 'indirect taxes' levied in economies based on a competititive market, and that, consequently, the Soviet net product, or national income, aggregate is on a market price basis, in contrast to the western National income aggregate which is on a factor cost basis. Soviet economists hold the view that 'turnover taxes' constitute part of the undistributed factor income of social production.

Estimates of the USSR national income prepared by USA scholars have been rejected as 'estimates . . . which will not bear the slightest criticism' [25]. The following estimates of USSR national income, in absolute figures, appeared for the first time in [41, p. 263]. These estimates were prepared by the statistical office of the United Nations on the basis of an item which appeared in Izvestia, and the index numbers published in Narodnoe Khozyaistvo [61].

USSR National Income (Net Material Product)
at 1960 prices, in 1000 million new rubles

Year	1000 million new rubles	Year	1000 million new rubles
1950	54	1955	93
1951	61	1956	103
1952	67	1957	110
1953	74	1958	124
1954	83	1959	133

D. THE INTEGRATION OF THE USSR NATIONAL ACCOUNTS WITH THOSE OF SNA

The basically different economic structure and systems, and the different theoretical and methodological approach to the calculation of the national income make a complete integration of the USSR national income accounts with SNA hardly possible.

I

In order to bring out the problems involved, it suffices to show the changes which would be required for the integration of the 'domestic product' account and the 'national income' account.

The SNA domestic product and national income accounts as reproduced in Appendix A to this section will be used as a basis from which to proceed with the problems of integration.

The economy would have to be divided into the following four sectors:

(a) Enterprises producing social products.
(b) Enterprises providing services, and private non-profit institutions.
(c) General government.
(d) Households.

Sectors (a) and (b) together would constitute the enterprise sector as defined in SNA, plus the private non-profit institutions which in SNA are part of the households sector. General government is assumed to be largely similar to that of SNA. Households sector is limited to the population in its capacity as consumers only. Households in their capcity as producers or providers of services would be included in sectors (a) and (b) respectively.

The first aggregative account to be discussed is that of domestic product. Net domestic product at factor cost (item 1.1 in SNA) would have to be expanded as follows:

Net domestic production of social products		x
Gross domestic social product	x	
Less intermediate goods	x	
Net domestic provision of services		x
Net domestic production of social products and		
services at factor cost		x
		x

The USSR concept of gross product is gross in the sense that it includes the intermediate products. It is also gross of depreciation.

In the suggested integration, the gross production would be only gross of the intermediate goods. The details of intermediate goods used up in production are recorded in the USSR accounts, and it would therefore not involve any problem for the USSR. It would however constitute a problem to some western countries and to most developing countries. Not all western countries would be in a position to find each year all the data for this expanded item. Only those countries which each year prepare appropriate input output tables would have available the required estimates for the intermediate products. All western countries would encounter some difficulty in separating social products from services.

The imputed net rent of the houseowners for the houses occupied by them, and the imputation of charges for the services of financial intermediaries would have to remain declared differences. The differences could be made explicit in a subitem to the aggregate of net domestic provision of services.

Provisions for domestic fixed capital consumption (item 1.2 in SNA) would have to be expanded as follows:

Depreciation of fixed assets of social producers					x
,,	,, ,,	,,	,, service enterprises		x
,,	,, ,,	,,	,, General Government		x
,,	,, ,,	,,	,, dwellings owned by population		x
Depreciation of domestic fixed capital					x

The above breakdown of the provisions for domestic fixed capital consumption is connected with the subdivision of the gross domestic fixed capital formation.

Western economies encounter many difficulties in the preparation of the estimates of fixed capital consumption. The preparation of separate flows for the provisions for fixed capital consumption as shown above would add more difficulties. The compilation of more detailed statistical data in Western economies would not only mean additional resources for this purpose, but also more information from the enterprises concerned who are not always anxious to render it.

As remarked before, the main difficulty in interpreting the USSR accounts in Western terms lies in the problem of the valuation of goods and services. The presentation of the net domestic product in the form suggested above leads to an aggregate of net domestic product of social products and services at factor cost. While the words 'at factor cost' describe this aggregate in a non-planned economy, they would not reflect the position in a planned economy. Except for a certain quantity of agricultural produce, prices for all other goods and services in a planned economy are determined by the appropriate planning boards. There is therefore no conceptual difference in the USSR between market prices and factor costs.

So much for the cost side of the social product. Let us now turn to the expenditures on the social product. Private consumption expenditure (item 1.5 in SNA) would have to be divided into purchases of goods from socially productive enterprises, and purchases of services from service enterprises. A precise distinction between consumption of goods and consumption of services would involve some statistical difficulties in western economies.

General Government consumption expenditures (item 1.6 in SNA): the subdivision of the consumption into goods and services would have to be on the same lines as in private consumption.

Gross domestic fixed capital formation (item 1.7 in SNA) would have to be divided into productive and non-productive capital and according to ownership as follows:

Gross fixed capital formation in social productive enterprises	x
„ „ „ „ „ service enterprises	x
„ „ „ „ „ General Government	x
Increase in dwellings of population	x
Gross domestic fixed capital formation	x
	x

It should be recalled here that according to the USSR concepts of 'value originated' and 'value realized', the prices for consumer goods and services may be fixed higher than cost by levying turnover taxes and other minor taxes higher than the normal profits for producer goods. The aggregate value of the gross domestic product of goods and services would, for internal USSR accounting purposes, not be disturbed. There would be an overvaluation of consumer goods counterbalanced by the undervaluation of producer goods. The values of the subaggregates would, however, not be comparable with those of western countries.

Increase in stocks (item 1.8 in SNA) would have to be divided into increases in producers' stocks, increases in stocks of service enterprises, and increases in stocks of general government.

Some of the flows in the domestic fixed capital formation (fixed assets and increases in stocks) are known to be defined differently in the USSR. These differences could result in lower government consumption expenditures and higher increases in government fixed capital formation, or items to be included in increases in stocks would be included in increases in fixed assets.

Exports and imports of goods and services (items 1.9 and 1.10 in SNA) would have to be separated into flows of goods and flows of services. The services part would have to include a subflow of the income or payment to the rest of the world on account of interest and dividends. The inclusion of this subflow of 'services' would make the domestic product account a semi-national product account from the point of view of the Western world. The net factor income from the rest of the world (item 2.10 in SNA) would consist of labour income only.

The valuation of exports and imports to and from the Western world would have to be shown by USSR in accordance with the actual (fob or cif basis) prices paid or received by USSR. This would mean a diversion from the USSR practice according to which the exports and imports are recorded in the Redistribution Fund at the actual prices paid or received but charged or credited to the other accounts as per prices centrally determined. The differences are the gain or loss to the Redistribution Fund.

The integrated national income account would be regarded by USSR national accountants as a 'national income from social production and services' account. This account would include 'primary incomes' and 'redistributed income'. The following problems would be involved in integrating the SNA national income account with USSR accounts.

Compensation of employees (item 2.1 in SNA) would have to be divided into compensation by social production enterprises, and compensation by services enterprises. Each flow would have to include explicitly or by definition the social insurance payments which are not part of employees compensation in the USSR.

Income from unincorporated enterprises (item 2.2 in SNA) would also have to be divided into social production and services. The former would in the USSR include the income of independent artisans and individual farmers, while the latter would include the income of those engaged in liberal professions.

Saving of corporations (item 2.4 in SNA) would have to be divided into savings of social producers and savings of service enterprises. The flows in the USSR accounts would, however, not be strictly comparable with the analogous Western flows. The profits of USSR enterprises are fixed by central planning, either directly, or indirectly by determining the prices centrally.

Apart from the fact that the direct taxes on corporations (item 2.8 in SNA) would have to be subdivided in a manner analogous to the other flows, it should be recalled that in addition to these taxes there are also the turnover taxes (net of subsidies) which the socialist productive enterprises and the service enterprises have to contribute to the Redistribution Fund.

The above are some of the changes which would be necessary for an integration of SNA and USSR accounts. While such changes would not involve particular difficulties to the USSR where practically all the statistical data are most probably available, it would in many instances be difficult for Western countries to compile the data and make the necessary estimates. But disregarding these 'technical' difficulties, there still remains the main problem of the unavoidable differences due to the problems of the price determination and the evaluation of the costs of production. No recasting of accounts, we daresay, could bridge these differences.

E. UK AND USA NATIONAL INCOME FOR 1950 AND 1960 ARRANGED ACCORDING TO USSR CONCEPTS

The following tables of the United Kingdom and of the United States have been prepared on the lines of the USSR concepts. They are based on the limited data published in [37, 53 and 55].

The United Kingdom

Comparative Table of the national income for 1950 and 1960

		1950 £ million		1960 £ million	
I.	*Income originating in the 'social production sphere'*				
	Agriculture, forestry, and fishing	686		907	
	Mining and quarrying	413		656	
	Manufacturing	4,169		8,128	
	Construction	639		1,319	
	Gas, electricity and water	251		583	
	Transport and communication excluding passenger transportation	604		1,294	
	Distributive trades	1,661		2,869	
	Net income from rest of the world	382	8,805	179	15,935
	Less: Stock appreciation	587		97	
	Capital consumption	589	1,176	1,372	1,469
			7,629		14,466
	Residual error		+35		−193
			7,664		14,273

II. *Income originating in the*
    'non-productive sphere'

Insurance, banking, and finance	332		646	
Other services	1,249		2,349	
Public administration and defence	720		1,337	
Public health and educational services	357		887	
Passenger transportation	362		573	
Ownership of dwellings	367		795	
Domestic services to households	98		86	
Services to non-profit making bodies	63	3,548	118	6,791
Less: Stock appreciation	63		30	
Capital consumption	401	464	643	673
		3,084		6,118
Residual error		+14		−90
		3,098		6,028
Total		10,762		20,301

The above comparative table shows among other things that the income originating in the 'non-productive sphere' increased from 28·7% of the total national income in 1950 to 29·6% in 1960.

The following shows a subdivision of the United Kingdom national income of 1960 into 'primary income' and 'redistributed income' measured from the factor income side.

I. *Primary income*			*£ million*
Income from employment			10,629
Income from self-employment		1,650	
Gross trading profits of companies		2,515	
Gross trading surpluses of public corporations		522	
Gross profits of other public enterprises		177	
Rent		589	
		5,453	
Less: Stock appreciation	97		
Capital consumption	1,372	1,469	3,984
Net income from abroad			179
			14,792
Residual error and discrepancy in adjustment			−519
			14,273

II. *Redistributed income*			
Income from employment			4,482
Income from self-employment		357	
Gross trading profits of companies		1,093	
Rent		533	
		1,983	
Less: Stock appreciation	30		
Capital consumption	643	673	1,310
			5,792
Residual error and discrepancy in adjustment			+236
			6,028
		Total	20,301

The United States

Comparative Table of the national income for 1950 and 1960

I. *Income origination in the*	1950	1960
'social production sphere'	*$ billion*	*$ billion*
Agriculture, forestry, and fisheries	17,384	17,161
Mining	5,202	5,516
Contract construction	11,962	22,494
Manufacturing	74,800	121,544
Wholesale and retail trade	43,555	68,768
Transportation (excluding local and highway passenger transportation)	11,975	16,276
Utilities; electric and gas	3,836	8,499
Local utilities and public services	114	256
Hotels and lodging places	1,277	2,052
Business services n.e.c.	2,099	6,088
Miscellaneous repair services and hand trades	846	1,816
Engineering and other professional services	849	2,337
Federal government enterprises	1,879	3,527
State and local government enterprises	628	1,689
Rest of the world	545	2,280
	176,951	280,303

II. *Income originating in the*	1950	1960
'non-productive sphere'	*$ billion*	*$ billion*
Finance insurance and real estate	20,964	42,325
Local and highway passenger transportation	1,316	1,540
Telephone, telegraph, and related services	2,980	7,033
Radio, broadcasting, and television	311	822
Personal services	2,815	4,626
Private household	4,313	10,300
Commercial and trade schools and employment Agencies	201	257
Motion pictures	836	831
Amusement and recreation	732	1,681
Medical and health services	4,292	11,002
Legal services	1,622	2,827
Educational services, n.e.c.	1,088	2,685
Religious organizations	515 }	3,498
Non-profit membership organizations	843 }	
Federal – general government	10,703	21,612
State and local government	10,150	25,712
	63,681	136,751
Total	240,632	417,054

It appears from the above comparative table that the income originating in the 'non-productive sphere' increased from 26·5% of the total national income in 1950 to 32·7% in 1960.

The following shows a sub-division of the United States national income of 1960 into 'primary income' and 'redistributed income' measured from the factor income side.

		$ billion
I.	*Primary income*	
	Compensation of employees	205,557
	Proprietors income	35,084
	Corporate profits	35,143
	Net interest	4,519
		280,303
II.	*Redistributed income*	
	Compensation of employees	88,140
	Proprietors income	13,149
	Rental income of persons	11,685
	Corporate profits	9,883
	Net interest	13,894
		136,751
	Total	417,054

VIII · NATIONAL ACCOUNTS IN CONSTANT PRICES

A. THE NEED FOR A COMPREHENSIVE SYSTEM OF NATIONAL ACCOUNTS IN CONSTANT PRICES, AND THE BASIC PROBLEMS INVOLVED

The desire to present the national accounts in constant prices emanates from the basic need to compare the scope and the results of economic activity of one period with those of another period. It is only by comparison that one can judge whether any one activity in the economy brought about better or worse results to the sectors involved and/or to the nation as a whole. The simplest procedure to satisfy this need would be to compare the accounts in current values of the two or more periods as originally prepared. The analyst would however soon realize that such comparison is of limited value. It is limited because the components of the values – the quantities and the prices – are different in the accounts under comparison. For in every dynamic economy there are practically continuous changes in relative prices, in kind, and in quality of goods and services produced and consumed. Hence the need to have these accounts expressed in terms free from the influence of the inter-temporal changes in prices and quantities.

While the original motive for the presentation of national accounts in constant prices was the desire to compare the accounts of one period with those of preceding periods, it has during recent years been realized that such a presentation is also of primary importance in the analysis of future economic behaviour – in economic prognosis.

Comprehensive national accounts in constant prices, achieved by indexes specifically designed for this purpose, could also be of use in national balance sheets. It may be presumed that with the development and wider use of national balance sheets, the national accounts will become an inseparable link connecting balance sheets as at the beginning and end of given periods of time. National accounts in constant prices arranged in similarly defined and computed prices will be a great contribution to this end.

If the use of the national accounts is to be made possible for all the above purposes then the complete system of the national accounts has to be expressed in constant prices. This, however, would involve a number of conceptual and technical difficulties. The data shown in the domestic production, consumption, and capital formation accounts are all based on values of 'commodities' and therefore can in principle all be presented in constant prices. Such a basis cannot easily be found for the domestic factor incomes, the factor income from abroad, and the savings of the sectors. These flows cannot, consequently, be uniquely expressed in constant prices. This holds true also for the various transfers between the domestic sectors and the rest of the world.

B. THE FAMILIAR TYPES OF QUANTITY AND PRICE INDEXES AND THEIR EXTENDED USE FOR NATIONAL ACCOUNTS IN CONSTANT PRICES

Long before the introduction of systematic national accounts, statisticians had developed various indexes for the measurement of changes in the purchasing power of money, of changes in industrial production, and of changes in other economic transactions such as exports, imports, etc. Each of these indexes was normally constructed with a specific purpose and limited objective in view. The retail price (cost of living) index, for instance, has been designed to measure the changes in the prices of a specified list of goods and services which a certain group of households normally bought in some base period. It does not pretend to measure the changes of all consumers goods and certainly not all the services (direct and indirect) consumed by households, without differentiating their level of income, place of residence, etc. But the methods laid down for the construction of this index can in principle be extended to a value measurement of all goods and services, whether consumed by households, non-profit institutions, or general government. The values of all goods and services can in principle be regarded as the product of a price and a quantity and these components can consequently be used for the deflation of the current values of consumption flows into constant prices. The properties of the Laspeyres or Paasche formulae of aggregate index numbers for prices and quantities are in principle adaptable to all the commodities consumed and accumulated as shown in the national accounts. Some statistical problems would indeed arise in connexion with commodities which did not exist at all or existed in a different form in the base period.

The commonly accepted industrial production index, again, covers only mining and quarrying, manufacturing, construction, electricity, and gas. It is an index confined to the production of mainly material goods, excluding agricultural products. It does not measure the provision of services at all. However, the great ingenuity shown by statisticians in overcoming conceptual problems, such as choosing the weights and indicators for index numbers, and the methods developed for handling the problem of new products, or new models of existing products, and differences in location, have paved the way to revaluing all domestic production as shown in the national accounts at the prices of a base year.

It will be noted that the examples have all been taken for 'commodity' flows both sides of the gross domestic product. But the problems of price and volume in national accounts extend beyond commodity flows. There are also the factor incomes – domestic and from abroad – there are taxes – direct and indirect – subsidies, transfers of all sorts, etc. Could the comprehensive and interrelated statistical data provided by the national accounts in current values for the whole nation and for individual sectors be revalued in constant prices by existing quantity and price index methods? Before answering this question it would be desirable to recapitulate the major flows and aggregates for the national accounts in a manner relevant to the purpose in view.

C. COMMODITY, PARA-COMMODITY, AND NON-COMMODITY FLOWS AND AGGREGATES

The flows shown in the national accounts could be classified into three major groups: (a) the commodity group, (b) the para-commodity group, and (c) the non-commodity group. The commodity group consists of those flows which can be measured by the input and/or output volume, and by their prices. Goods and services consumed by private and government sectors, fixed capital formation, increase in stocks, exports and imports of goods, and non-factor services, could all be classified under the commodity group of flows. These flows are the components of the aggregate of total expenditures on gross domestic product at market prices. It has been pointed out that estimates of expenditure are usually made at market prices, i.e. prices which include the net indirect taxes. This is not only an easier method of estimating expenditures but it is also more meaningful, if the national accounts – in current and in constant prices – are to measure the welfare of the nation. It should however be noted that these commodity flows contain an element of a non-commodity flow, viz. net indirect taxes (indirect taxes less subsidies).

The gross domestic product aggregate is a commodity flow since it measures all the goods and services produced by the domestic industries. It is in fact a pure economic aggregate because estimates of production are usually made on a factor cost basis, i.e. not including net indirect taxes. It is true that to the extent that indirect taxes can be traced and attributed to the commodities upon which they were levied, they can be regarded as a commodity flow. But such tracing cannot always be completely achieved, either because indirect taxes are not always levied on specific commodities, or because they are not levied ad valorem. Net indirect taxes should therefore be regarded as a non-commodity flow.

The aggregate of gross domestic product at market prices and the aggregate of expenditures on gross domestic product at market prices may be classified as para-commodity aggregates for two reasons: (a) because their deflation can only be achieved by the summing up of the subflows and flows of which they are composed and each of which is deflated by its specific index, (b) because they contain the net indirect taxes flow which cannot always be considered as a commodity flow. The author would in fact classify all total aggregates, whether they are composed of commodity or non-commodity flows and aggregates or not, as para-commodity aggregates. He would also classify as a para-commodity flow any flow which though it is by itself a non-commodity flow, is identical with a commodity flow or aggregate. The gross domestic savings, for instance, though by itself a non-commodity aggregate, could nevertheless be classified as a para-commodity aggregate because it can usually be identified with the gross domestic capital formation aggregate which is a commodity flow.

There are again, flows recorded in the national accounts for which there are no unique accompanying commodities which could be expressed in quantities and in prices. These are the non-commodity flows. This group of flows consists of all the income flows, such as the compensation of employees, income from property, net factor income from abroad and all other components of the national income aggregate. All transfers between the various sectors, the sector savings (not to be confused with the total savings of the nation which were classified above as a para-commodity flow), the net loans to or from abroad also constitute part of the non-commodity flows group.

D. INDEXES FOR A COMPREHENSIVE SYSTEM OF NATIONAL ACCOUNTS IN CONSTANT PRICES

Social accountants have confined themselves to estimating only the gross domestic product account in constant prices. This account at factor cost consists of commodity flows, and as such can in principle be estimated in constant prices. In accordance with the two sides of this account they have adopted the following two general methods: (a) The production method according to which production – gross of amortization and at factor cost – originating in all industries (industries producing material goods and industries providing services) is added up and valued at base year prices. (b) The expenditure method according to which expenditures on final products – consumption, capital formation and net exports, are deflated at base year prices. If the constant prices according to the production method were estimated gross of the net indirect taxes, or, alternatively, if the revaluation according to the expenditure method were made at factor cost, the result achieved by these two methods would in principle be identical. In practice, however, it is difficult to achieve complete identity. The C.S.O. in [36, p. 39] points out that 'a detailed reconciliation of the two sets of results would be possible only if sufficient information were available to determine the contribution of each industry to each item of final expenditure. It would be necessary to have a very detailed input-output matrix for each year, in real terms.'

The statistical office of the United Nations requests that, for its statistical year book, data on the industrial origin of the gross domestic product be presented at constant factor cost, while the the data on the expenditures on gross national product is requested at constant market prices. These are independent data and cannot be used for an articulated system of national accounts in constant prices. A recent United Nations survey [50] shows that most of the reporting countries prepare their constant price estimates by industry on a factor cost basis, while the estimates by expenditure of all reporting countries are based on the market prices. The U.K., according to the same survey, is the only country which prepares the estimates by expenditure on both a market price and a factor cost basis. Since the estimates at constant prices of the expenditures on final products on a factor cost basis are made independently of the constant price estimates by industry at factor cost, they provide a way of checking the results.

For interspatial comparisons, particularly between planned and non-planned economies, there is good reason for having the gross domestic product aggregate separated into flows of material goods and non-factor services. Such a subdivision would also be useful in intertemporal comparisons in constant prices. A separation of the commodity flows into material goods and services would make it possible to make appropriate use of the index of industrial production which is no doubt more sound and stable than the index numbers constructed for the service industries.

Another point which should be raised here is the matter of provisions for domestic fixed capital consumption. As pointed out before, the deflation of domestic product is made gross of depreciation. If indexes are to be constructed for a comprehensive system of national accounts in constant prices, it would be necessary to have these provisions deducted from the gross domestic product. Furthermore, index numbers would have to be constructed for the provisions for domestic fixed capital consumption by the individual sectors. The reasons for having these provisions estimated on a replacement basis become still more substantiated when related to estimates in constant prices. The connotation of accounts in constant prices is a measurement in real terms. Depreciation estimated on a straight line basis or any other basis other than the replacement basis would be meaningless for accounts in constant prices.

Reference was made earlier to the technical advantage of arriving

K

at the expenditures on final products in constant prices from estimates at factor cost. It is also important to have these expenditures in constant prices at factor cost, if it is required to present the accounts of the individual sectors in constant prices. It is particularly important for the households sector account where the factor incomes are shown. Factor income should properly be estimated as identical with the net national product at factor cost.

The balancing of the expenditures on gross domestic product in constant prices involves the problem of adjustments for changes in terms of trade, or 'trading gain'. The surplus of exports over imports is not wholly due to relative increases in the respective quantities. In extreme cases the surplus of exports over imports (which is a component of the surplus of the nation in the current account) may be positive in current prices but negative in deflated values. The trading gain measures the gain derived (or loss sustained) by an open economy from the relative price changes of exports and imports. Since the surplus of exports over imports is a commodity flow, it can in principle be deflated. Social accountants are, however, divided as to whether it should be deflated by the smaller of current exports or imports or by current exports only.

So much for the gross domestic product account which, generally speaking, can be deflated on the basis of the commodity flows of which it is composed. The second general standard account of the national accounts, viz: the national income account, is of a different character in so far as constant prices are concerned. Its components are non-commodity flows. Indexes for non-commodity flows present special conceptual and technical problems. The C.S.O., in confining the discussion of the problem of indexes for non-commodity flows to income flows only, points out that 'It is impossible to make direct estimates in real terms of income as such for, until income is spent, it cannot be identified with actual goods and services, and all income is not necessarily spent. Further, there is no satisfactory way of valuing income from abroad in real terms' [36, p. 37]. Professor R. Stone in his discussion of the whole problem of presenting non-commodity flows in constant prices also notes that 'The search for deflators of these totals is essentially the search for appropriate collections of commodities on which these sums of money might be spent and in relation to the changing cost of which they can, in an interesting way, be expressed in real terms' [34, p. 90]. He further comes to the general conclusion that 'it is impossible to find a unique set of deflated values of the non-commodity transactions in an accounting system such that the accounts continue to balance in real terms' [34, p. 93]. Changes in non-commodity flows could, by implication, be measured only in an indirect way or in a non-unique manner. It would therefore be convenient to deflate the national income flows with the aid of the para-commodity aggregate of net national product at factor cost which is identical with the national income. It is true that the national product at factor cost also contains the net factor income from the rest of the world flow which is also a non-commodity flow. But the factor income from abroad, like the surplus of exports over imports, could be deflated by either the import or the export flows according to whether this income brought about larger or smaller exports. Alternatively the factor income from abroad could be deducted from the national income aggregate resulting in a domestic income to be deflated by the index number of the net domestic product at factor cost with which domestic income is identical.

Another method of inflation would be to deflate each income flow by the commodity flow to which it may be assumed to be mainly related. The compensation of employees total, or a major part of it, for instance, could be deflated by the index number of the private consumption expenditure at factor cost, while, for instance, the savings of the corporations flow could be deflated by the index number of the net domestic capital formation at factor cost. Net indirect taxes could be deflated pro rata to government consumption and government financing of increase in capital formation.

The above method if adopted for non-commodity flows other than national income components would, incidentally, accentuate the necessity of differentiating between current and capital transfers between sectors and from abroad. While current transfers would have to be deflated by a consumption flow, capital transfers would have to be deflated by a capital flow.

An original method of balancing a system of national accounts in real terms was recommended by R. W. Burge and R. C. Geary [49]. The method is based on the logical assumption that 'If the constant price series is conceivable it should bear a close formal resemblance to the current price series, if only because in the base year the current price and constant price systems must be identical'. [19, p. 4]. The whole national accounts system has been consolidated into five equations, in an articulated form, with nine variables representing the flow and aggregates contained in this consolidated system. Since five of these variables, viz: gross domestic product, consumption, capital formation, exports and imports can be uniquely deflated, the deflated values of the other four flows can also be established.

To achieve the proposed balancings of the accounts in constant prices, the authors had to restrict the deflation to gross product thereby avoiding the problem of deflating the various transfers, and to adopt 'particular definitions of items like savings (S) which are not uniquely deflatable' [19, p. 4]. In the five equations mentioned above, savings are equal to capital formation plus the surplus of exports over imports. The figure does not include the net factor income from abroad.

The methods recommended would need further empirical study by statistical offices which are in a position to compile all the required data. After some experiment with actual figures, it should be possible to find a way to construct appropriate index numbers for a comprehensive and articulated system of national accounts. Certain agreed conventions, as are typical of other conceptual problems in national accounts, will certainly have to be adopted.

Appendix 'A' to Chapter Two

SNA STANDARD ACCOUNTS

Account 1 – Domestic Product

	£			£
1.1 Net domestic product at factor costs (2.9)	485	1.5 Private consumption expenditure (4.1)		325
1.2 Provisions for domestic fixed capital consumption (3.4+4.14 +5.17)	25	1.6 General government consumption expenditure (5.1)		110
1.3 Indirect taxes (5.8)	15	1.7 Gross domestic fixed capital formation (3.1)		60
1.4 *Less* Subsidies −(5.2)	−10	1.8 Increase in stocks (3.2)		30
		1.9 Exports of goods and services (6.1)		10
		1.10 *Less* Imports of goods and services −(6.4)		−20
Gross domestic product at market prices	515	Expenditure on gross domestic product		515

Account 2 – National Income

	£		£
2.1 Compensation of employees (4.7)	380	2.9 Net domestic product at factor cost (1.1)	485
2.2 Income from unincorporated enterprises (4.8)	45	2.10 Net factor income from the rest of the world (6.2)	−7
2.3 Income from property (4.9)	40		
2.4 Saving of corporations (3.3)	8		
2.5 Direct taxes on corporations (5.9)	5		
2.6 General government Income from property and entrepreneurship (5.6)	5		
2.7 *Less* interest on the public debt (5.7)	−3		
2.8 *Less* interest on consumers' debts −(4.2)	−2		
National income	478	Net National product at factor cost	478

Account 3 – Domestic Capital Formation

	£		£
3.1 Gross domestic fixed capital formation (1.7)	60	3.3 Saving of corporations (2.4)	8
3.2 Increase in stocks (1.8)	30	3.4 Provisions for fixed capital consumption in corporations (1.2*)	15
		3.5 Net capital transfers to corporations (5.14+6.8−4.15)	−4
		3.6 Net borrowing of corporations −(4.17+5.19+6.11)	−4
		Finance of gross capital formation in corporations	15
		3.7 Finance of gross capital formation in non-corporate private sector (4.12)	109
		3.8 Finance of gross capital formation in non-corporate public sector (5.13)	−34
Gross domestic capital formation	90	Finance of gross domestic capital formation	90

Account 4 – Households and Private Non-Profit Institutions

Current Account

	£			£
4.1 Consumption expenditure (1.5)	325	4.7 Compensation of employees (2.1)	380
4.2 Interest on consumers' debt −(2.8)	2	4.8 Income from unincorporated enterprises (2.2)	45
4.3 Direct taxes (5.10)	35	4.9 Income from property (2.3)	40
4.4 Other current transfers to general government (5.11)	5	4.10 Current transfers from general government (5.3)	2
4.5 Current transfers to rest of the world (6.5)	9	4.11 Current transfers from rest of the world (6.3*)	11
4.6 Saving (4.13)	102		
Disposal of income	478	Income of households and private non-profit institutions	478

Capital Reconciliation Account

	£			£
4.12 Finance of gross capital formation in non-corporate private sector (3.7)	109	4.13 Saving (4.6)		102
		4.14 Provisions for fixed capital consumption (1.2*)		5
		4.15 Net capital transfers from corporations (3.5*)		2
		4.16 Net capital transfers from government (5.15)		−3
		4.17 Net capital transfers from rest of the world (6.9)		2
		4.18 Net borrowing −(3.6+5.19+6.11)		1
Disbursements	109	**Receipts**		109

Account 5 – General Government

Current Account

	£		£
5.1 Consumption expenditure (1.6)	110	5.6 Income from property and enterpreneurship (2.6)	5
5.2 Subsidies −(1.4)	10	5.7 *Less* intreest on the public debt (2.7)	−3
5.3 Current transfers to households (4.10)	2	5.8 Indirect taxes (1.3)	15
5.4 Current transfers to rest of the world (6.5)	4	5.9 Direct taxes on corporations (2.5)	5
5.5 Saving (5.16)	−57	5.10 Direct taxes on households (4.3)	35
		5.11 Other current transfers from households (4.4)	5
		5.12 Current transfers from rest of the world (6.3*)	7
Disposal of current revenue	69	Current revenue	69

Capital Reconciliation Account

	£		£
5.13 Finance of gross capital formation in non-corporate public sector (3.8)	−34	5.16 Saving (5.5)	−57
5.14 Net capital transfers to corporations (3.5*)	−3	5.17 Provisions for fixed capital consumption (1.2*)	5
5.15 Net capital transfers to non-corporate private sector (4.16)	−3	5.18 Net capital transfers from rest of the world (6.10)	3
		5.19 Net borrowing −(3.6+4.18+6.11)	9
Disbursements	−40	Receipts	−40

Account 6 – External Transactions (Rest of the World Account)

Current Account

	£			£
6.1 Exports of goods and non-factor services (1.9)	10	6.4 Imports of goods and non-factor services −(1.10)	20
6.2 Net factor income from rest of the world (2.10)	−7	6.5 Current transfers to rest of the world (4.5+ 5.4)	13
6.3 Current transfers from rest of the world (4.11+5.12)	18	6.6 Surplus of nation on current account (6.7)−	12
Current receipts	**21**	**Disposal of current receipts**	**21**

Capital Reconciliation Account

	£		£
6.7 Surplus of nation on current account (6.6)	−12	6.11 Net lending to rest of the world −(3.6+4.18+5.19)	−6
6.8 Net capital transfers from rest of the world to corporations (3.5*)	1		
6.9 Net capital transfers from rest of the world to households (4.17)	2		
6.10 Net capital transfers from rest of the world to general government (5.18)	3		
Receipts	**−6**	**Disbursements**	**−6**

Note: An asterisk denotes 'part of' item listed.

APPENDIX B

GLOSSARY OF SYMBOLS USED IN CHAPTER TWO

C_h – Private consumption expenditure

C_p – General government consumption expenditure

C – Total consumption expenditures

D – Provisions for domestic fixed capital consumption

D_e – Provisions for fixed capital consumption in corporations

D_n – Provisions for fixed capital consumption in households

D_p – Provisions for fixed capital consumption in government

Dis   – Statistical discrepancy

F_h – Finance of gross capital formation in non corporate private sector

F_p – Finance of gross capital formation in non-corporate public sector

GDP_f – Gross domestic product at factor cost

GDP_m – Gross domestic product at market prices

GNP_f – Gross national product at factor cost

GNP_m – Gross national product at market prices

GI   – Gross domestic capital formation

IF   – Gross domestic fixed capital formation

IS   – Increase in stocks

ISA   – Inventory valuation adjustment

L   – Lending or borrowing

M – Import of goods and services

M^1 – Imports of goods and services and income payments to rest of the world

NI   – Net domestic capital formation

NDP_f – Net domestic product at factor cost

NNP_f – Net national product at factor cost

NNP_m – Net national product at market prices

RC   – Interest on consumers' debt

RP   – Interest on public debt

S   – Total savings

S_e – Savings of corporations

S_h – Savings of households

SN   – Surplus of nation on current account

S_p – Saving of government

SU   – Subsidies

T   – Direct taxes on households

TE   – Direct taxes on corporations

TI   – Indirect taxes

TR   – Current transfers

TRC   – Capital transfers

X   – Export of goods and services

X^1 – Export of goods and services and income receipts from rest of the world

Y   – National income (same as NNP_f)

YH   – Personal income

YHD	– Disposable income of persons	YL^1	– Disbursements of wages and salaries
YI	– Households, etc., income from property $(=YI^1+YI^{11}+YI^{111}+YI^{1v})$	YL^{11}	– Other labour income
		YL^{111}	– Employer contribution for social insurance
YI^1	– Households, etc., income from rent	YL^{1v}	– Excess of accruals over disbursements of wages and salaries
YI^{11}	– Households, etc., income from interest		
YI^{111}	– Households, etc., income from dividends	YP	– General government income from property and entrepreneurship
YI^{1v}	– Corporate transfer payments to households, etc.	YRW	– Net factor income from the rest of the world
YL	– Compensation of employees $(=YL^1+YL^{11}+YL^{111}+YL^{1v})$	YU	– Income from unincorporated enterprises

CHAPTER THREE

Input - Output System

I · BACKGROUND AND THE CLOSED MODEL

Each generation produces its outstanding interpreters of the accumulated inheritance of art and human thought. These interpreters superimpose 'variations' of their own which are adapted to the needs and taste of their age. The 'variations' of such interpreters in the sphere of economics have either been such as to expand and deepen analytical thought, or such as to provide empirical grounds for some existing economic theory.

Wassily W. Leontief is one of the most remarkable interpreters of economic thought in this generation. His greatest contribution has been in the form of an empirical application of equilibrium analysis presented in his work *The structure of American economy* [27]. Leontief and his followers consider themselves as walking in the footsteps of Francois Quesnay and Leon Walras. According to Schumpeter [33, p. 240], Quesnay, again, was greatly influenced by Cantillon. The line of thought could no doubt be traced still further if the footsepts were not marred by time.

While Quesnay appears to have had some indirect and general influence upon Leontief's empirical research work, Walras' influence has been more direct. In the words of J. R. Boudeville [3] 'Wassily Leontief est, en effet, un économiste disciple de Walras et admirateur de Quesnay'. This will also be apparent in the following brief presentation of Leontief's original closed model study given in [27].

The foundation upon which Leontief's empirical study is based is that there exists a general interdependence between the various parts of an economy. This is the very idea emphasized by the physiocrats. The problem to which Leontief has tried to give an empirical solution is one that Walras and his Lausanne school have tried to demonstrate and solve in hypothetical quantities. It is the problem of general equilibrium.

The original study of Leontief, which later became popular under the name of the closed model of the input-output system, will be taken first. It divided the economy into various industries each of them having an output (production) taken up by other industries and each of them requiring inputs (consumption) from other industries of the economy. The households sector has also been considered as one of the industries; the output of the households industry consisting of its labour, capital, and entrepreneurial services, while its input is comprised of the final goods and services purchased from the other industries. This obviously implied that there was a connexion between a households' factor incomes and its expenditures on final goods and services. Government activity and trade with the rest of the world have also been regarded as separate industries and treated similarly to the 'household industry'. There was no final demand in this model. All consumption was regarded as an intermediate process for further production.

A basic and critical assumption was made in connexion with the technical input-output relationships between all these industries. It was assumed that specific doses of input are required for the output of each industry. If one of the industries is to produce a certain specified output of goods or services it requires certain specified quantities of input from some or all the other industries. Any required increase in the output of the industry, again, brings about a relative increase of inputs from the other related industries. These interindustrial technological relationships, or 'coefficients of production' are also assumed in the open model and will be discussed in the following subsection.

II · MAJOR CHARACTERISTICS
OF THE OPEN MODEL

The outstanding feature of the open model in contrast with the closed model is the line drawn between processing industries on the one hand and the so-called 'final bill' sectors on the other hand. The economy is divided into two major parts. One part – the 'closed' part – consists of the industry groups all performing processing activities which are considered to be functionally related to one another, while the other part consists of sectors of the economy which though related to the industries are not functionally dependent upon them. Differently put: one part consists of the industries which are interconnected with regard to the intermediate goods and services they receive from and supply to one another; the second part consists of the sectors from whom the industry groups purchase labour services and other 'primary inputs', and to whom they sell their outputs of final goods and services. The sectors whose inputs are the final goods and services provided to them by the industries group and whose outputs are labour and other 'primary inputs' are largely those known to us from the national accounts systems. The households, the government, and the rest of the world sectors constitute the major part of these sectors outside the industrial boundary. The 'input and output' of these exogenous sectors are determined autonomously by factors outside the 'closed' production system. In addition to these three sectors there is also the 'investors sector', i.e. the sector absorbing the gross capital formation of the economy. The final goods and services absorbed by all these sectors are commonly referred to as the 'final bill', while the services which they provide are frequently called 'primary inputs'.

By separating the final sectors from the processing industries the open model has achieved the following three major advantages over the closed model.

a. Sectors with less stable interindustrial relationships were separated from industries with more stable interindustrial relationships. The outputs (labour) of the households, for instance, cannot very well be regarded as determined by its inputs (consumption), as the output of say, the coal mining industry is dependent upon its inputs from the mechanical engineering or the iron and steel industries.

b. While the closed model could only determine the structure of an economy, the processing industries in the open model are determined with regard to scale as well as to structure. The given final bill of the exogenous sectors determine the scale of the physical outputs, and the fixed labour wages set the scale of prices.

c. The system became more useful for planning purposes because of the possibility of analysing the relationship between all the processing industries and the sectors of the final demand. This will become evident from our later discussion of the coefficients of direct and indirect requirements per unit of final demand.

The following scheme of an input-output table of the open model type should help in the further examination of the underlying basic concepts and the methodological structure of the input-output system.

It will be observed that the scheme is divided into two major parts which correspond to the sectoring of the economy as outlined above. There is first the part where the flows of the intermediate goods and services between the processing industries are shown. Each industry is given a row and a column in this square 'chessboard' matrix. The values recorded in the row are those of the goods and services provided by the industry to the other industries, while the values in the columns are those of the goods and services taken in from the other industries.

In addition to the 'chessboard' matrix where the endogenous inter-industrial flows are recorded, there are: (a) columns to the right-hand side where sales constituting final demand of the autonomous sectors are carried, and (b) rows below, where purchasers of primary inputs from the autonomous sectors are recorded. In the final column the total output, i.e. the output of each industry to the various industries and to the 'final bill', is recorded, while in the final row the total input, i.e. the inputs purchased by each industry from the other processing industries and from 'primary inputs' is recorded.

L

Columns for origin of inputs \ Rows for disposition of outputs	Industry 1	Industry 2	Industry 3	$\cdots$	$\cdots$	Industry n	Total intermediate output	Final bill	Total output
Industry 1	—	x_{12}	x_{13}	$\vdots$	$\vdots$	x_{1n}		Y_1	X_1
„ 2	x_{21}	—	x_{23}	$\vdots$	$\vdots$	x_{2n}		Y_2	X_2
„ 3	x_{31}	x_{32}	—	$\vdots$	$\vdots$	x_{3n}		Y_3	X_3
....	$\vdots$	$\vdots$	$\vdots$	$\vdots$	$\vdots$	$\vdots$		$\vdots$	$\vdots$
....	$\vdots$	$\vdots$	$\vdots$	$\vdots$	$\vdots$	$\vdots$		$\vdots$	$\vdots$
Industry n	x_{n1}	x_{n2}	x_{n3}	$\vdots$	$\vdots$	x_{nn}		Y_n	X_n
Total intermediate input									
Primary inputs									
Total input									

Attention should be drawn to the fact that there is no intra-industry flow shown in the industry groups matrix of the above scheme. The output of one establishment sold to another establishment within the same industry is not shown. It is 'free from duplication'. The principle diagonal of the intermediate product flow matrix is, consequently, left blank. The United Kingdom reason for omitting the intra-industry flow is that 'measuring the total value of the output of the different industry groups free from duplicating makes it independent of the structure and organization of the industry group and of the number of establishments in the industry for which returns are made' [38, p. 1]. Those favouring the inclusion of intra-industry flow point out that the co-efficient of production in a matrix showing intra-industry flow would be smaller and theoretically preferable to a co-efficient of production based on a matrix with no intra-industry flow. This argument is relevant in an economy where some of its major processing industries are themselves using up significant quantities of their products. It should be noted that the figures compiled for the census of production would normally include all sales of one establishment to another within the same industry. The problem of an intra-industry flow matrix versus a blank diagonal matrix could therefore best be decided according to the industrial structure of the country. The procedure adopted varies in fact from one country to another.

An intermediate product flow matrix with an intra-industry flow would take on the following form:

$$
\begin{array}{ccccc}
x_{11} & x_{12} & x_{13} & \cdots\cdots & x_{1n} \\
x_{21} & x_{22} & x_{23} & \cdots\cdots & x_{2n} \\
x_{31} & x_{32} & x_{33} & \cdots\cdots & x_{3n} \\
\cdots\cdots & \cdots\cdots & \cdots\cdots & \cdots\cdots & \cdots\cdots \\
\cdots\cdots & \cdots\cdots & \cdots\cdots & \cdots\cdots & \cdots\cdots \\
x_{n1} & x_{n2} & x_{n3} & \cdots\cdots & x_{nn} \\
\end{array}
$$

III · INDUSTRIES – CONSTITUTION AND CLASSIFICATION

It has already been indicated that the open model first sectorizes the economy into two broad parts. One part consists of the industry groups, while the other part consists of the 'final bill' group. These two parts are further subdivided.

An industry in this system is understood to be a group of enterprises in the economy performing a certain processing activity. The cost structure of this process of production must be similar for all the establishments within this industry group, and the products produced by it must be homogeneous. These are two essential prerequisites for the input-output system. Statistically they are the most difficult aims to achieve. The simplest and statistically the most convenient method would be to adopt the enterprises as a basic unit. This would, however, lead to a great variety of productive output being treated as a homogeneous output and would consequently make it difficult to justify the fixed co-efficients of production which are highly controversial. The accepted method has therefore been to consider the 'establishment' as the basic unit of an industry. Establishments are defined as being the smallest possible units of sufficiently similar productive characteristics for them to be grouped together for analytical purposes. The common characteristics of establishments may differ. They may produce similar end commodities, or use similar materials in production, or may employ similar technological processes.

The need to group establishments by their common characteristics is clearly due to limitations in the very concept of co-efficients of production. Sound co-efficients of production can be established in the manufacturing industries, in mining, or in gas and electricity where the inputs and outputs are more or less clearly cut. But when the concept is extended to agriculture, to government, or to other services, it becomes more difficult to group the establishments on common characteristics. These difficulties are not peculiar to the co-efficients of production in the input-output system. They are encountered in the search for appropriate net output quantity indicators for the construction of indexes for industrial production. An assumption is made there that the commodity inputs into industries are proportional to commodity outputs, and then a single indicator either of the gross output or of any one commodity input serves as an indicator of the net output of an industry.

An establishment determined as above may still produce some products which are secondary to its principal product. It is the principal product of the establishment, determined usually on the basis of the proportion of the gross value of the product, i.e. the product which constitutes the largest part of the sales, that decides in what industry the establishment is to be included.

Grouping establishments into industrial groups also raises the problem of the number of industries the model is to include. There can be no absolute and universal rule about this. It is however obvious that the larger the number of industries, i.e. the smaller the aggregation, the more stable are the co-efficients of production. On the other hand, too large a number of industires may lead to a situation where there would be too much repetition of products. Under such circumstances the stability of the co-efficients of production would be weakened. The problem of the number of industries to be included is closely connected with what are recognized to be the two major shortcomings of the production function assumed in the static open input-output model. The first shortcoming lies in the assumption that the input pattern of an industry is not dependent on the output. In other words, there is no substitution among inputs once the level of output of the industry is given. This is contrary to the commonly accepted economic theory according to which the doses of each input applied in producing a given output are not constant and will vary according to the changes in the relative prices of the input doses and according to any technological changes which may take place. The second shortcoming lies in assuming that the so called 'product mix' does not vary. The problem of deconsolidation or overaggregation of establishments would not arise if each industry contained establishments whose products are identical in all respects. In fact, however, very few industries can be so ideally constituted. Industries in an input-output model will contain establishments with non-identical technical methods or with dissimilar technical requirements. Only by assuming a constant product mix, i.e. by assuming that when the output of one of the products of an industry changes, the outputs of all its other products will change in the same proportion, can we argue that output uniquely determines the inputs of an industry with dissimilar products and technical conditions.

The brunt of such criticisms, which are theoretically well-grounded could be met by the least possible aggregation of industries. The larger the number of the industries included in the model the smaller would be the possibilities of having diversified products within each industry. In aggregating establishments and industries, the aim should be in fact to achieve the maximum degree of homogeneity of products within each industrial group. It would not however seem advisable to subdivide the economy to such an extent that the output of many establishments would be attributable to several industry groups which would in turn entail extensive splitting of inputs.

The size of the model would largely be determined by the pattern, i.e. variety of products, of the major industries in the country concerned. Only empirical studies can decide how many industries are necessary to provide an analytically useful model.

Studies so far made have also shown that classification of the industries is not, and probably cannot be uniform for all countries. The industries whose transactions are of major importance to the country concerned will be the most disaggregated, and vice versa. The availability of the huge amount of information required is another factor in classification. In the United Kingdom Input-Output tables for 1954, for instance, the classification of industries 'was determined largely by the information readily available' [38, p. 3]. This is evidently true for other European countries, as is confirmed by the Economic Commission for Europe which reported 'that input-output compilations are essentially dependent on the basic sources of national statistics, comparatively little data in any country being collected directly for this purpose' [48, p. 50].

IV · VALUATION OF PRODUCTION

Before proceeding with the 'final bill' stage of the input-output scheme, the valuation of production must be discussed. There are two aspects of this problem. There is first the basic necessity of expressing the production of the industries in definite units. The other aspect of the problem is connected with the inter-industrial flow of the products. In other words, should production be valued at the prices of the selling or of the purchasing industry?

Theoretically, there is no reason why the input-output table should not wholly or partly be constructed in physical units. Measurements in physical units would for some purposes be preferable to measurement in monetary units. The frequent need for price adjustments, for instance, would thereby be avoided. An input-output table could be constructed in terms of quantities of physical homogeneous commodities where each unit of quantity would represent an amount that can be purchased for one unit of money. In practice, however, an input-output table based on physical units is almost impossible. The adoption of such a method would require a classification of industries for each reasonably homogeneous commodity. Such a splitting is not only, as indicated, impossible in practice, but also impractical for most analytical purposes. It must also be remembered that the value of the production of some industries can only be expressed in monetary units. Another great advantage in using monetary units is that it enables us to add up all the inputs (the columns) as well as all the outputs (the rows) of each industry. In view of these advantages, and in view of the fact that the production statistics readily available are generally expressed in monetary units, it is generally accepted that the flows should be recorded in current monetary values. Robert Dorfman indirectly criticized this accepted procedure of valuation. He argued that

since the raw materials are the outputs of supplying industries there is, at first glance, a direct connexion between the level of activity in any industry and the levels in its supplying industries. At second glance, though, the connexion is not quite so direct (even apart from the inventory problem), for, purely as a matter of technology, inputs (except for services) must be produced before they can be used. Consequently the technological relationships (except for service inputs) connect the current level of each industry with previous levels of its supply industries and subsequent levels of its customer industries [11, p. 123].

Because of these timing problems 'a few countries have also prepared tables in terms of the prices of an earlier year rather than in current prices' [44, p. 11]. The monetary unit weight for the processing industries actually plays a technical role only. It is mainly a matter of statistical convenience and it is decided upon accordingly. It has been for instance suggested that the prices for an input-output table in a centrally planned economy could be 'the accounting prices used in estimating plan fulfilment' [48, p. 47].

The other, complementary valuation decision to be made is connected with the difference between the so-called 'producers' valuation' or 'sellers' valuation', and the 'purchasers' valuation'. Statistics showing the cost of an industry's products only up to the point when they are sold to another processing industry or final consumer are called the 'producers' valuation' statistics. By contrast, statistics showing the cost of an industry's products up to the point where they reach an industry or a final buyer purchasing these products are called the 'purchasers' valuation' statistics. The difference between these two valuations consists mainly of the marketing margin, the transportation costs and the net indirect taxes. By recording inter-industrial transactions on a producers' valuation, the flow of distributive services will be from the distributive industries to the processing industries, i.e. as an ouput of the former and an input of the latter. When recording sales to the final buyers on a producers' valuation, the distributive services would also appear as a separate part of the value of the commodity purchases from the distributors. An illustration is given in [7, p. 9]

. . . a consumer who purchases, for example, a bar of soap at a retail store is shown as if he paid directly to the manufacturer the manufacturer's selling price for the soap and then paid to the transportation, storage, and trade industry . . . the amount of wholesale and retail trade margins, transportation, and other distribution costs. Taxes levied after the manufacture of the soap was completed are shown as a separate payment as are taxes or customs duties on imported goods.

The recent tendency has been to employ the producers', or sellers', valuation in the setting up of a matrix of inter-industrial flow of production. The reason given in [38, p. 2] in favour of this valuation is 'that the figure of sales to both industries and to final buyers within each row are on the same price basis and are, as far as possible, directly comparable'. Another reason given by Evans and Hoffenberg is that

In a producer's value table explicit account can be taken of differential trade or other margins by type of consumer. For example, distribution costs for a product entering foreign trade may be quite different than for the same item entering domestic consumption. Notably domestic excise taxes on tobacco and alcoholic beverages would not be levied on export shipments.

Evans and Hoffenberg also point out at the same time the disadvantages in using the purchaser's valuation. They argue that

in a purchaser's value table, all distribution costs for a sector's output will appear in its input structure, and again distributed through its output allocations. Input ratios will thus be based on an output total which includes distribution costs for the sector's production. But these costs in turn will depend on the output distribution itself, which may be quite variable from year to year.

Hence, estimates based on purchaser's value introduce a source of instability in input structure which can be avoided by using producer's values. [13, p.103].

Those favouring the purchasers' valuation would point out that the readily available statistics are in terms of the prices paid by the buyers of the products. Additional information and data are therefore needed to eliminate distribution costs. Another argument, put forward in [44, p. 17], is that 'for most input-output studies it is a distinct advantage to have final expenditures already expressed at buyer's prices because they are then in agreement with the expenditure at market prices comprising final demand in the national income accounts, and the necessity for charging consumers, etc., with a separate large total for distribution costs is eliminated'. It would seem that when a country is in a position to prepare input-output tables in addition to the national accounts it would be important from a statistical point of view to have different estimates for both systems so that there is a possibility of checking one against the other. Moreover, it would be an advantage to be able to arrive at the national income aggregate directly from the final net product flows at factor cost and not only from the factor income flows. It is only when a country does not prepare intput output tables that it is advantageous and convenient to have final expenditure estimated at market prices.

The estimates at sellers' valuation would also make it possible to provide data for Table II in SNA, which shows industrial origin of gross domestic product at factor cost. This table is important for economic analysis in western countries and can play an important role in recasting the national accounts system for use by centrally planned economies or for comparison with their national accounts.

V · THE FINAL BILL

In the input-output scheme given at the beginning of this chapter there is only one column for the 'final bill'. In practice, however, this column is usually divided into several columns for the final bill or autonomous sectors. Typical autonomous sectors are consumers, government, investors, inventory changes, and exports. These will be examined in the above order.

In the consumers' sector column are normally recorded all expenditures on goods and services by households and private non-profit institutions serving households. The distribution of consumers' expenditure, which should be parallel to the classification of the industries in the input-output table provided, generally involves some difficulties. These are unavoidable in those cases where the producers' valuation is used, and the estimates of these expenditures are then prepared on a double basis. Part of the estimates are made

by working back from the expenditures to the output of the industries, while another part is obtained by estimates of the industries'
output for personal consumption. Finally efforts are made to adjust
the figures of consumption of households on a current market price
basis as estimated for the national accounts. There is no such problem involved when the valuation is on a purchasers' basis.

Expenditures on goods and services by government – central and
local – are included in the government column. The problem of
allocating these expenditures according to the classification of the
industries is generally solved in a fashion similar to that applied for
the households sector.

A basic principle in the construction of an input-output table of
the static open model type – in contrast with the proposed principles
for a dynamic model – is to segregate the current accounts transactions from the capital transactions. Capital investments are generally not made each year in a stable proportion to the activity of the
same year. To include the investment expenditure in the inter-
industrial flows would mean the derivation of a co-efficient of
production based partly on capital inputs which were specific only
to the year for which the input-output table was prepared. Furthermore, the main interest in inter-industrial relations is focussed on
current transactions. Consequently, all fixed capital expenditures
are carried to the exogenous sector of investors, implying of course,
that their pattern is determined by autonomous policy decisions.

In estimating the fixed investments, it is attempted, as it was for
the estimates of households consumption, to adjust them to the
fixed capital formation aggregates in the national accounts of the
country – both in valuation and in the definitions of fixed capital.

Net changes in inventory such as raw materials, goods in process,
and finished goods are included in an input-output table in order to
allow for that part of the current production which has not yet been
sold to consumers or investors, or for that part of the production of
previous years which has been put in for further processing. Taking
this flow into account makes it possible to determine the quantities
which have actually been used up in inter-industrial activity, and

not merely the purchases and sales during the current year. By employing the 'use' concept, another element of stability is introduced in the co-efficient of production. Practical difficulties are, however, encountered in replacing the purchases and sales flow by the amounts actually absorbed in production by each industry. Statistics are commonly adjusted so as to show in the inventory change the fall or rise in inventories irrespective of their location or ownership.

The problem of valuation of changes in stock has been discussed in connexion with the national accounts concepts. It will be recalled that the principle recommended, for instance, by SNA, is that the value of changes in stock be calculated as the difference between gross additions to stocks during the reported period valued at purchase price or cost, and gross withdrawals from stocks valued at the prices current when the withdrawals are made. This would measure the change of stock at current replacement cost. This recommended principle probably ought to be more rigorously applied in the open model. In practice, however, the principle is not adhered to because of the statistical difficulties. The change in stock is, instead, estimated as a sum of physical changes each multiplied by an average of prices prevailing during the period.

Different ways of recording the changes in inventory have been adopted. In the United Kingdom inter-industrial relations tables for 1954 [38] the increase in the value of stocks (finished goods) and work in progress is entered in a final demand column (input), while the increase in value of stocks of (raw) materials and fuel is entered in a row as a negative input. 'Sales by final buyers for scrap' is entered as a primary positive input for the purchasing industries and as a negative input of the 'final buyers' column. In the United States [13] – additions to inventories are shown as an input in a final bill of goods column, whereas depletions of inventory are entered in a primary output flow. The procedure adopted by Canada [6] and [7] is to enter the value of physical changes in (all types of) inventories in a final demand column; additions to inventories are in positive figures, whereas depletions are in negative figures. The different methods were adopted in order to reach a more stable co-efficient of production. It is by empirical observations that the most suitable method for each country can be selected.

Exports of goods are mostly entered according to the industries which are the final manufacturers of the exported goods. An exported commodity, the final producing process of which is performed in two or more industries, is entered as the output of the major producer. Exports of services are entered in the service industry groups.

It is common practice to evaluate exports on a f.o.b. basis. Since valuation in the input-output tables is, as already indicated, sometimes made on a sellers' basis and sometimes on a buyers' basis, adjustments have to be made to arrive at a consistent valuation.

In the United Kingdom, where valuation is on a sellers' (producers') valuation

exports are valued, as far as possible, at sellers' price; a more or less arbitrary deduction is made to the f.o.b. value to convert them to this basis. The difference between the f.o.b. value and sellers' price is regarded as an export by the services industry group. [38, p. 20].

The same procedure has been adopted in the United States [13, p. 109].

The analysis of the final bill of goods sectors has been on the basis of the breakdown accepted by several countries. It should, however, be pointed out that the final bill of goods column is not always subdivided in the above fashion. In the United Kingdom inter-industry relations in 1954, for instance, the bill of final goods consists of two columns only, viz: (a) Increase (change) in value of stocks and work in progress, and (b) final buyers, which is an aggregate of consumers, public administration, domestic gross fixed capital formation, and exports of goods and services.

VI · PRIMARY INPUTS

The primary inputs row of the scheme is sub-divided into several other rows. These inputs usually consist of the compensation of employees, income from investments, capital consumption allowances, net indirect taxes, and imports. These will be examined in that order.

The compensation of employees row is also referred to in the input-output system as the households row. The compensation includes wages, bonuses, premiums to pension funds, and all other grants and fees. In addition to all wages, etc. it includes, as in the national accounts system, the employers as well as the employees' contributions to social insurance.

The income from investments row contains in addition to interest and rent received by households all incomes of unincorporated enterprises, and the net profits of private and public corporations.

The capital consumption allowance, being the allowance for the fixed assets which were used up in the course of production during the current year, should in principle be calculated on a replacement value basis. The necessity of adhering to the principle of providing for fixed capital consumption on a replacement basis has been discussed at length in Chapter II which deals with the national accounts system. In the input-output system the necessity is still more absolute. In this system where the emphasis is on the physical process of production, and where the inputs and outputs could be expressed in physical units, the monetary equivalent must definitely be computed on a replacement basis. In periods of increasing stocks and changing prices, only a replacement basis reflects the physical capital consumption.

The above three rows, viz: compensation of employees, income from investments, and the capital consumption allowance, are aggregated in the United Kingdom Inter-industry relations in 1954 [38] into one row named 'Gross Domestic Income' which also includes values for 'stock appreciation'. The United Kingdom statistics, as indicated in the section on the comparison of the national accounts system in various countries, prepare separate estimates for the differences between the book value changes and the physical changes of finished goods and works in progress which are due to fluctuation in prices.

Net indirect taxes are not always included among the autonomous rows. An example in point is [7] where net indirect taxes are included in the inter-industry flow matrix. Moreoever, there are two rows for this item within the inter-industry flow matrix. One row contains 'Indirect taxes on imported goods and services', while the other row is for 'indirect taxes less subsidies on domestic goods and services'. Imports of goods and services are also recorded within the inter-industry flow matrix. This procedure raises the total value of the inter-industry flow matrix to a market price level. Where net indirect taxes are entered as an autonomous row the total value in the inter-industry flow matrix is on a factor cost basis. The valuation of production in the Canadian input-output table mentioned above is on a 'sellers' basis. In the United Kingdom inter-industry relations in 1954 [38] net indrect taxes (taxes on expenditure less subsidies) are entered as an autonomous row – indirect taxes being a positive input, and subsidies a negative input.

The treatment of imports is also not uniform in all countries. For input-output purposes, imports are divided into two categories. One category consists of the so-called competitive imports. These are imported goods which are also produced domestically; the second category consists of non-competitive imports, i.e. imported goods which are not produced in the importing country. Because of the areas of possible substitution it is not easy to make such clear distinctions, and the division, if it is indeed made, is made in an arbitrary manner. This is unfortunate because different recording of competitive and non-competitive imports results in different co-efficients of production, particularly where the competitive imports are in significant quantities.

In some input-output tables, as for instance in [13], the non-competitive imports are entered in an autonomous row as direct inputs of the industries where they were first purchased. The competitive imports, on the other hand, are entered as inputs of those industries where the counterpart domestic products are produced, and at the same time, also recorded as additional output of the industries. This method makes the cost structure of the industry producing such goods dependent on the quantity of goods imported. While this may not be of great significance in the United States where such imports have no great weight, or in other countries where competitive imports are stable, it may become a serious shortcoming for those countries where these quantities are significant and/or unstable. It should be pointed out that the US method of recording competitive imports is consistent with its method of recording at producers' valuation. We have seen that under producers' valuation there is no direct link between the producer and the buyer in so far as the margin of trading and transportation costs are concerned. Recording the competitive imports in the imports row as an input of the industry which produces the counterpart domestic products and then entering them as its output to the industry which uses them, gives in a sense a distributor status to the industry which produces the counterpart domestic products, in addition to its being also a domestic producer.

In the United Kingdom inter-industry relations of 1954 [38], all imported merchandise – competitive and non-competitive, as well as that which is later re-exported – has been entered in an autonomous row distributed as primary inputs of the industries purchasing these goods. Imported goods which undergo no further processing in the United Kingdom, and re-exports, are charged as an input of the final buyers.

Just as the total final bill of goods column agrees with the gross national expenditures, so, in an analogous manner, the total primary inputs coincide in most cases with the gross national product at market price. The total value of primary inputs is consequently equal to the total final bill of goods.

VII · CO-EFFICIENTS OF DIRECT
AND INDIRECT REQUIREMENTS PER UNIT
OF FINAL DEMAND

Input-output tables of the static open model type which have been prepared in course of the last two decades by practically all industrially developed countries, themselves represent a detailed statistical picture of the industrial interrelationship. At the same time they also show the interdependence between the industrial groups and the final bill sectors. The preparation of such a 'tableau économique' can in itself be of great value in the observation and study of various phenomena of economic activity. A comparison of such static tables for various periods could show the direct effect which an expansion or contraction of final demand might have upon the productive structure of the industry providing it. Such tables show, for instance, how many housing units the housing industry has provided to the 'final bill' sectors. They also show the units of input the housing industry had to draw from the brick industry and from the cement industry etc. in order to provide this number of housing units. One could therefore also learn from these tables the direct relationship between the number of output units of the housing industry and the number of input units the housing industry had to obtain for this purpose from the other related industries and from the 'primary input' sector. Such direct relationships, which are known as the co-efficients of production, can also provide insight into the effects of expansion in the industry concerned. If, for example, the housing industry has to expand its production in order to meet an increase in the demand for housing, it is possible to calculate the additional units of input it will have to draw from other industries and from 'primary input' sectors. Since these tables similarly provide information about the kind and number of units of input the brick and cement industries require for their output, the co-efficients of production of these industries make it possible to calculate the number of additional units of input they will require in order to provide the increased quantities of output the housing industry requires from them. This was possibly the original aim in compiling statistics on inter-industrial relationships. However, the data as applied in the input-output system soon became an important theoretical as well as a forceful practical tool for central planning and decision making. By tracing the direct effect which an increase in demand for housing had on the industries immediately related to the housing industry one soon realizes that this increase

M

has set off a long series of reactions in an ever-increasing number of industries which are not directly related to the housing industry. These direct and indirect repercussions may become weaker for industries far removed from the housing industry, but they will nevertheless still be felt by them. Furthermore, this wave of reactions may eventually return to the housing industry, because some of the other industries, and perhaps even the housing industry itself, may need more housing for the increased labour force required to satisfy the increased demands for their product.

The open model of the input-output system aims then to show both the direct and the indirect impact which any change in a final demand can have upon all the productive activities of the economy. This implies that, if the final bill is given as a goal, or plan, the model might be capable of predicting the whole level of production of the economy. In other words, in addition to their use as a social accounting system, the input-output tables take on the characteristics of a current econometric model.

Reverting to the open model scheme given above it will be of interest to show the mathematical process for obtaining the co-efficients representing the combined direct and indirect inputs required for each specified unit of final demand. It is by means of these 'co-efficients of direct and indirect requirements per unit of final demand', that the 'ex-post' figures of the input-output tables acquire the ability to make forecasts.

Assuming the economy is divided into four industries, the following four linear equations will represent their outputs to one another, their output to the 'final bill' sectors, and their total outputs.

Set I

$$
\begin{aligned}
- \quad +x_{12} +x_{13} +x_{14} +Y_1 &= X_1 \\
x_{21} \quad - \quad +x_{23} +x_{24} +Y_2 &= X_2 \\
x_{31} +x_{32} \quad - \quad +x_{34} +Y_3 &= X_3 \\
x_{41} +x_{42} +x_{43} \quad - \quad +Y_4 &= X_4
\end{aligned}
$$

A general notation for the above equation would be: x_{ij} denoting the output of industry i to industry j; Y_i – the output of industry i to the final demand sectors; and X_i – the total output of the i'th industry.

Replacing each input of an industry by its co-efficient of production, the mathematical expression of which is

$$a_{ij} = \frac{x_{ij}}{X_j},$$

the linear equations of Set I would take on the following form:

Set II

$$
\begin{aligned}
- \quad a_{12}X_2 + a_{13}X_3 + a_{14}X_4 + Y_1 &= X_1 \\
a_{21}X_1 \quad - \quad + a_{23}X_3 + a_{24}X_4 + Y_2 &= X_2 \\
a_{31}X_1 + a_{32}X_2 \quad - \quad + a_{34}X_4 + Y_3 &= X_3 \\
a_{41}X_1 + a_{42}X_2 + a_{43}X_3 \quad - \quad + Y_4 &= X_4
\end{aligned}
$$

In matrix notation the above equations could be expressed as $AX + Y = X$, where A denotes the matrix of the input co-efficients.

The equation in Set II can also be expressed in the form of the following matrix and two vectors:

Set III

$$
\begin{bmatrix}
I & -a_{12} & -a_{13} & -a_{14} \\
-a_{21} & I & -a_{23} & -a_{24} \\
-a_{31} & -a_{32} & I & -a_{34} \\
-a_{41} & -a_{42} & -a_{43} & I
\end{bmatrix}
\begin{bmatrix}
X_1 \\
X_2 \\
X_3 \\
X_4
\end{bmatrix}
=
\begin{bmatrix}
Y_1 \\
Y_2 \\
Y_3 \\
Y_4
\end{bmatrix}
$$

In matrix notation, the above equations could be expressed as $(I - A)X = Y$. An inversion of this expression is $(I - A)^{-1}Y = X$.

By having the matrix in Set III above represent the determinant of co-efficients of production $-D-$, and denoting the algebraic complements (minors) by D_{ji}, then the inversion of Set II could be expressed in the following four equations.

Set IV

$$\frac{D_{11}}{D}Y_1 + \frac{D_{21}}{D}Y_2 + \frac{D_{31}}{D}Y_3 + \frac{D_{41}}{D}Y_4 = X_1$$

$$\frac{D_{12}}{D}Y_1 + \frac{D_{22}}{D}Y_2 + \frac{D_{32}}{D}Y_3 + \frac{D_{42}}{D}Y_4 = X_2$$

$$\frac{D_{13}}{D}Y_1 + \frac{D_{23}}{D}Y_2 + \frac{D_{33}}{D}Y_3 + \frac{D_{43}}{D}Y_4 = X_3$$

$$\frac{D_{14}}{D}Y_1 + \frac{D_{24}}{D}Y_2 + \frac{D_{34}}{D}Y_3 + \frac{D_{44}}{D}Y_4 = X_4$$

Denoting $\frac{D_{ji}}{D}$ by A_{ji}, Set IV can be expressed in the following inverted matrix of $(I-A)$ and the two vectors of the final demand and the total output respectively.

Set V

$$\begin{bmatrix} A_{11} & A_{21} & A_{31} & A_{41} \\ A_{12} & A_{22} & A_{32} & A_{42} \\ A_{13} & A_{23} & A_{33} & A_{43} \\ A_{14} & A_{24} & A_{34} & A_{44} \end{bmatrix} \begin{bmatrix} Y_1 \\ Y_2 \\ Y_3 \\ Y_4 \end{bmatrix} = \begin{bmatrix} X_1 \\ X_2 \\ X_3 \\ X_4 \end{bmatrix}$$

The inversion of the matrix $(I-A)$ provides a set of co-efficients which represent the combined direct and indirect requirements of input per unit of the final demand. The sum of the products of each of the elements in a particular row by the final sales of each industry provides the total requirements of the industry in the particular row.

The computations of the co-efficients of direct and indirect requirements per unit of final demand are made on the basis of the statistical figures of a given period. These co-efficients can however be applied for later periods as long as it may be assumed that no changes in the cost structure have taken place, i.e. as long as the co-efficients of production have not changed.

It should be remarked here that the computation of an inverted matrix is a very laborious job. It is only with the aid of the electronic computer that the input-output system can be taken into consideration as a practical method of social accounting.

A vast literature of theoretical and empirical studies on the input-output system has sprung up during the last decade. The above discussion was centred on the rationale of the open model, the technique involved, and the points at which the input-output system meets the national accounts. These points are the main concern here. The fact that the final demand is the equivalent of the expenditure on gross domestic product and that the primary inputs are the equivalent of the gross domestic income in the national accounts system is of importance in the discussion which follows later of the integration of the input-output system with the national accounts. There remain some flows such as the factor incomes from abroad, the various transfers between the sectors of the economy and net lendings, which are outside the sphere of the input-output system and unique to the national accounts system.

VIII · APPLICATIONS

In concluding this discussion of the open model it is worth indicating some of its applications.

Inter-industrial relationship, the synonym for the open model, has the important connotation that the economy must be more or less industrially developed. This should be emphasized before proceeding with the following list of applications of the open model. A country which is industrially underdeveloped and depends mainly upon its agricultural industry will have little use for the model if only for the reason that the co-efficients of production of primitive agricultural techniques are extremely unstable, being dependent on the weather conditions and corresponding changes in the crops. The applications cited are, then, mainly relevant to industrially developed economies.

The previous discussion of the co-efficients of direct and indirect requirements per unit of final demand has shown how it is possible to derive from the model the level and structure of production corresponding to a given final demand. The open model can predict the production requirements which are necessary to sustain a given or planned demand. By no other existing technique could all the direct and remotely indirect requirements to sustain a certain final demand be determined. The final demand is estimated or specified independently of the industrial input-output relationship. This of course holds true under the assumption that all the relevant forces in the future will be similar to those in the past.

The model can be conveniently used to determine what expansion of domestic production and imports would be required to carry out a certain investment programme such as a large housing scheme or other projects on a national scale. In fact even an input-output model of a relatively large degree of aggregation of domestic production could be of great help for such investment projects. Such an application is very useful to the public policy of all countries at all times. It is particularly important for developing countries and in times of emergency.

The open model can be used to trace the whole output of an industry to the element of final demand in which this output is embodied. In other words it can be shown, for instance, how much steel was bought by consumers, government, investors, and exports while buying all other final products. Such information is of course very useful for industrial decision-making since industry is thereby in a position to know where its final market actually is.

The input-output open model can also be usefully applied in the investigation of regional development as against national development. In geographically large countries with substantial differences in income levels, technical methods of production, consumption behaviour, etc., the model can be adapted to take account of the regional aspects of production and demand.

Finally, where the data for the input-output tables are compiled in conjunction with the work on the preparation of the national accounts, and more particularly the domestic product account, the data of the latter is bound to be on a sounder basis.

CHAPTER FOUR

Flow of Funds Systems

I · ORIGINS AND ADAPTATIONS

Quantitative data were compiled in the thirties in several countries mainly with the intention of measuring the money and credit circuit in terms of the equation of exchange in a transactions velocity sense. Enthusiasts for the famous $MV = PT$ equation were trying to give it an empirical basis. Aggregates were consequently constructed to show the relation between the quantity of money and the price level. As with all non-interrelated aggregates these aggregates could be relied upon only for a partial analysis of the economic and financial interplay between some of the transactors and only for part of the transactions of the national economy. The data so compiled, particularly in the United States, seemed to be in search of some framework where the available flow and aggregate could be put together.

In 1944 Wesley C. Mitchell prepared an unpublished memorandum where he laid down the basic concepts of a social accounting structure for the interdependent measurement of the flow of payments and receipts in a monetary economy. In the same year Professor Morris A. Copeland was invited by the National Bureau of Economic Research 'to direct an exploratory project to determine what could be done to provide a fuller statistical picture of the money circuit' [10, p. 3]. In his study, Professor Copeland set out a conceptual approach to a detailed accounting framework for money flows, and he also compiled the appropriate data for the United States for the years 1936–47 [10]. Reference will be made later to some of the concepts and structural fundamentals of this study, and more particularly to those which have since been changed.

Encouraged by the above work the board of governors of the federal reserve system of the United States decided to continue with the study of the 'flow of funds' (in contrast to Copeland's 'money-flows'), and in 1948 accordingly instructed its division of research and statistics 'to develop a national flow of funds accounting system which could be kept up to date on a regular basis.' [45, Preface]. The concepts and methods of this system together with the relevant data, and the sources for the material, were laid down in 'Flow of funds in the United States 1939–53' [56]. The federal reserve system continued to develop the system with a view to maintaining the data on a current quarterly basis so that it could be more useful to the central bank and for all other analytical work on financial and economic interactions. It also considered some conceptual and structural changes mainly in order to lay more stress on investment and savings statistics and to bring them out more clearly. Later a revised version of the flow of funds system appeared in the Federal Reserve Bulletin for August 1959 [57].

It should immediately be pointed out that in no country outside the United States has the system of flow of funds been put in operation in a manner similar to that adopted by the federal system. 'Financial analysis' data and more consistent and integrated studies are being prepared by several industrially developed countries, but not in the form of an independent framework. Graeme S. Dorrance of the international monetary fund in [12] has made a study of the various national statements and accounts of financial and related statistics being prepared by seventeen such countries, including the United States. The material being prepared by these countries 'includes a wide range of studies, extending from simple statements of the factors causing changes in deposit money bank reserves, to statements covering the full range of financial transactions in an economy, with data on physical investments frequently incorporated with financial entries' [12, p. 7]. A few studies which resemble the flow of funds system have not only less detail, but are also closely connected or actually combined with the national accounts system of the country. They are not an independent set of accounts and do not constitute a separate system of social accounts.

It would seem that the lack of enthusiasm about following the flow of funds system in the manner presented in the US is largely due to the fact that the theoretical background of the system is not self sustained enough. The system in many respects follows the method used for the analysis of economic activities and not financial ones. A system for the analysis of financial transactions must have an independent approach to the financial behaviour of the transactors, to the classification of the transactors, and to the choice of the financial and related transactions. Expert groups of the conference of European statisticians have devoted several sessions to the problem of formulating an accounting system of financial transactions and financial assets and liabilities. The proceedings have been briefly summarized in [46] and [47]. The development of an appropriate framework for the analysis of financial transactions still requires independent academic study before it can be handled by technical experts.

While this study will mainly be devoted to the examination of the flow of funds system, it will also cursorily examine the national transactions accounts for Canada, and the French expanded accounts, which include financial transactions accounts.

II · SOME CONTRASTS BETWEEN THE FLOW OF FUNDS SYSTEM AND THE NATIONAL ACCOUNTS SYSTEM

The flow of funds system, as already intimated, tries to link financial transactions and the financial structure of the economy with non-financial transactions and the productive structure of the economy. This at least seems to be the ideal towards which the system is aiming.

A clearer insight into the role which the flow of funds system is to play in the study and analysis of the financial transactions in an economy can conveniently be provided by showing some of the contrasts between this system and the National Accounts system.

The flow of funds accounts shows distinctly the purchase and sale of existing assets, since such transactions involve the receipt and payment of money or decrease (increase) in the credit (debit) balances of the transactors. National accounts which are designed to show the production of goods and services during a given period of time would not be concerned with the details of these transactions. On the other hand, there is no room for imputed incomes in the flow of funds system. Clearly if an employee receives part of his income in the form of food or housing there is no money transaction involved and consequently such transactions do not find their way into the flow of funds accounts. In the national accounts system such imputed incomes are recognized and recorded.

The national accounts system is essentially concerned with the measurement of the final achievement of an economy in the field of production within a given period of time. National accounts show how and to what extent the fruits of this productive achievement were distributed among those taking part in the production and other members of the economic society, what part of the products has been consumed within the same period, and what was left (saved) in the form of capital goods to be used in the coming periods for consumption or further processing. All this information could to a great extent be obtained in physical terms. The flow of funds system, on the other hand, aims first to measure the flow of money and credit and all other financial media from one group of trans-actors to another in the economy with a view to demonstrating how the producers, consumers, and acquirers of wealth have financed their respective activities during the given period. Another task, mainly assumed in the new version of the flow of funds system, is to show the status of the financial assets and liabilities of these producers, consumers, and institutions at certain intervals of time. Professor Copeland has described the national accounts system as a system which 'tells us something about how well our economy works', as compared with the 'moneyflows' accounts which 'help us to understand how our economy works' [10, p. 61].

It should be noticed that in the national accounts the emphasis is on the functions of production or consumption or acquisition of capital; in the flow of funds system the accent is on the ownership of the means of production or of the financial assets. The invariance to ownership in the national accounts system is one of the major and basic conceptual differences between the latter and the flow of funds system.

The following hypothetical financial statements, though extremely simplified, may throw more light upon the aims of the flow of funds system as compared with those of the national accounts system.

Let us assume an economy which consists of a household providing all the required labour for the economy and also consuming all its products, a producing enterprise, and a bank which performs the tasks of a central bank, a mortgage bank, and a commercial bank. The balance sheets as at the beginning and end of a certain period, as well as the receipts and expenditures during the period of the units of the economy as assumed above, are shown below.

HOUSEHOLD (CONSUMER)
BALANCE SHEET AS AT BEGINNING OF YEAR

Assets	£	Liabilities	£
Cash on hand (currency)	3	Net worth	95
Cash with bank (demand deposit)	12	Mortgage indebtedness	45
Capital assets (non-financial)	100		
Shares and debentures	25		
Total	140	Total	140

RECEIPTS AND DISBURSEMENTS
(SOURCES AND USES OF FUNDS) DURING THE YEAR

Disbursements (Uses)	£	Receipts (Sources)	£
Consumption	185	Income from wages	200
Repayments a/c of mortgage	15	Sales of shares and debentures	5
Added to deposit with bank	4		
Added to cash on hand	1		
Total	205	Total	205

Within the year amounts have clearly been withdrawn from or deposited with the bank by the consumer. He has increased or reduced his cash on hand from time to time. The amounts shown are only the net additions of cash on hand and in the bank by the end of the year. This also goes for the stock and debentures. The consumer might have sold and repurchased various financial instruments during the year. The entry shown indicates the net amount by which his portfolio has been reduced by the end of the year.

BALANCE SHEET AS AT END OF YEAR

Assets	£	Liabilities	£
Cash on hand (currency)	4	Net worth	110
Cash with bank (demand deposit)	16	Mortgage indebtedness	30
Capital assets	100		
Shares and debentures	20		
Total	140	Total	140

ENTERPRISE (CORPORATE BUSINESS)
BALANCE SHEET AS AT BEGINNING OF YEAR

Assets	£	Liabilities	£
Cash on hand (currency)	9	Net worth	120
Cash with bank (demand		Loan payable (commercial	
deposit)	16	loan)	35
Plant and equipment	120		
Material stock (inventory)	10		
Total	155	Total	155

RECEIPTS AND DISBURSEMENTS
(SOURCES AND USES OF FUNDS) DURING THE YEAR

Disbursements (uses)	£	Receipts (sources)	£
Wages	200	Sales	185
Added to cash on hand	2	Increase in loan payable	3
		Decrease in demand deposit	14
Total	202	Total	202

The note to the receipts and disbursements of the household concerning the gross flow during the year, and the net resulting flow by the end of the year holds also here with regard to the cash on hand and in the bank, as well as for the commercial loan.

It is assumed that in addition to the cash sales the enterprise also increased its material stock (inventory) by a sum of £10.

BALANCE SHEET AS AT END OF YEAR

Assets	£	Liabilities	£
Cash on hand (currency)	11	Net worth	115
Cash with bank (demand deposit)	2	Loan payable (commercial loan)	38
Plant and equipment	120		
Material stock (inventory)	20		
Total	153	Total	153

BANK
BALANCE SHEET AS AT BEGINNING OF YEAR

Assets	£	Liabilities	£
Mortgage loans	45	Net worth	55
Commercial loans	35	Deposit accounts	28
Shares and debentures	15	Obligation for currency	12
Total	95	Total	95

RECEIPTS AND DISBURSEMENTS
(SOURCES AND USES OF FUNDS) DURING THE YEAR

Disbursements (uses)	£	Receipts (sources)	£
Decreases in deposits	10	Decrease in mortgage loan	15
Purchase of shares and debentures	5	Increased obligation for currency	3
Increases in commerical loans	3		
Total	18	Total	18

It will be noticed that it was assumed that no salaries were paid; no bank charges (actual and/or imputed) made, and no interest (actual or imputed) was paid or received.

BALANCE SHEET AS AT END OF YEAR

Assets	£	Liabilities	£
Mortgage loans	30	Net worth	55
Commercial loans	38	Deposit accounts	18
Shares and debentures	20	Obligations for currency	15
Total	88	Total	88

Of all the above financial statements the national accounts system would be concerned only with those showing the receipts and expenditures. Furthermore, it would limit itself only to the data on production, consumption, and capital formation, or the resulting savings during the year. These transactions would be shown in the national accounts as follows:

DOMESTIC PRODUCT

	£		£
Gross domestic product	195	Private consumption	185
		Increase in stock	10
Total	195	Total	195

DOMESTIC CAPITAL FORMATION

	£		£
Increase in stock	10	Saving of households	15
		Saving of enterprises	−5
Total	10	Total	10

HOUSEHOLDS – CURRENT ACCOUNT

	£		£
Consumption expenditure	185	Compensation of employees	200
Savings	15		
Total	200	Total	200

The accounts of the flow of funds system as derived from the above financial statement would be as follows:

HOUSEHOLDS – SUMMARY OF FLOW OF FUNDS

Uses	£	Sources	£
Acquisition of financial assets:		Gross saving	15
Increase in cash (currency) £1		Decrease in financial assets: Sale of shares and debentures	5
Increase in demand deposit 4	5		
Decrease in liabilities: —			
Decrease in mortgage loan	15		
Total	20	Total	20

HOUSEHOLDS – STRUCTURE OF FINANCIAL ASSETS AND LIABILITIES AT END OF YEAR

Assets	£	Liabilities	£
Cash on hand (currency)	4	Mortgage indebtedness	30
Cash with bank (demand deposit)	16		
Shares and Debentures	20		

ENTERPRISE – SUMMARY OF FLOW OF FUNDS

Uses	£	Sources	£
Capital expenditure		Gross saving (dissaving)	−5
Change in inventories	10	Increase in liabilities	
Acquisition of financial assets		Increase in commercial loans	3
Increase in cash (currency)	2	Decrease in financial assets	
		Decrease in demand deposits	14
Total	12	Total	12

ENTERPRISE – STRUCTURE OF FINANCIAL ASSETS AND LIABILITIES AS AT END OF YEAR

Assets	£	Liabilities	£
Cash on hand (currency)	11	Commercial loans	38
Demand deposits	2		

BANK – SUMMARY OF FLOW OF FUNDS

Uses		£	Sources		£
Acquisition of financial assets:			Decrease in financial assets:		
Purchase of shares and debentures	£5		Decrease in mortgage loans		15
Increase in commercial loans	3	8	Increase in liabilities:		
Decrease in Liabilities: —			Increase in obligation for currency	£3	
Decrease in deposits (Enterprises)	14		Increase in deposits (households)	4	7
	Total	22		Total	22

N

BANK – STRUCTURE OF FINANCIAL ASSETS
AND LIABILITIES AS AT END OF YEAR

Assets	£	Liabilities	£
Mortgage loans	30	Deposit accounts	18
Commercial loans	38	Obligations for currency	15
Shares and debentures	20		

It will be noted that the 'structure of financial assets and liabilities' as at the end of the year for each of the three assumed units in the economy differs from the balance sheets as at the beginning of the year by the fact that the former include neither the non-financial assets on the assets side nor the 'net worth' on the liabilities side. The 'structure of financial assets and liabilities' consequently does not balance. The fact that these statements do not include the non-financial assets needs no special explanation here. As to the 'net worth' item it should be realized that it is a residual balance and may include not only shares but also various surpluses and reserves. In any case 'net worth' in the balance sheet of a household is no more than a technical necessity in a double entry system of accounts and consequently of no financial interest to the economy. Moreover, shares cannot be regarded as any other financial obligation of a company to outsiders. Shares are closely related to the value of the company's assets – non-financial as well as financial. This latter point will be taken up again later when the flow of funds transactions categories are analyzed.

III · SECTORING IN THE UNITED STATES FLOW OF FUNDS SYSTEM

An industrially developed country is usually recognized by its complex financial structure. The structure and number of the financial institutions of a country is an indication of its general level of economic development. The flow of funds system of the United States categorically assumes an economy with a financial system by and through which the various transactors are encouraged or discouraged to do or undo various economic activities. By deciding to reduce or increase the holdings of capital assets of financial instruments, the owners of these assets, mainly through appropriate financial intermediaries, shift from one to another their purchasing power, their savings or dissavings. The flow of money and credit is a reflection of the large variety of decisions taken to carry out current transactions, and to plan future undertakings. In sharp contrast to the input-output system and in contrast to the national accounts where the sectoring is on a functional basis, i.e. transactors performing homogeneous economic functions, the flow of funds sectoring is on an institutional basis. A firm may be constituted of several establishments which for input-output purposes would be grouped in different industries, but in the flow of funds sectoring they would all be included in the firm which makes the financial decisions and carries out the financial transactions for all its establishments. Such decisions in such an economy are greatly dependent upon the respective decisions of the various financial institutions through which most of the funds are channelled. The flow of funds system therefore divides the economy mainly into ownership and decision making entities. It is also because of the important, and often controlling, if not decisive role, which the financial institutions play in determining the income level at which the decisions made by those willing to invest and those willing to save will coincide, that the flow of funds system singles them out as separate and distinct sectors.

The flow of funds system divides the economy into ten domestic sectors and an additional rest of the world sector.

i. *Consumers and Non-Profit Organizations.* Included in this sector are persons in their capacity as members of households and personal trusts. All consumer transactions – non-financial and financial – of households as well as of farm business, and non-farm, non-corporate business, are recorded in this sector. All expenditures for the purchase of new and old houses for the owner's occupancy, and the cost of maintaining these homes are recorded in this sector. On the other hand, lessorship activities of households in their capacity as land-lords are excluded from this sector. These activities and all the other business activities of households are recorded in the farm and non-corporate business sectors respectively. Non-profit organizations are included in this sector because of a lack of the statistical data required to separate the transactions of these organizations from those of consumers. In the original accounts set up by the federal reserve system [56] these organizations were included in a sector called 'Other Institutional Investors'. The inclusion of the non-profit organizations in the consumers' sector makes the consumers' sector in this system more similar to the households sector in the national accounts system. Professor Copeland in his study of money-flows included these organizations in the sector of unincorporated 'Business Proprietors and Partnerships et al' [10, p. 45].

ii. *Farm Business.* Grouped into this sector are all farms, whether unincorporated farm enterprises or corporate farms. It also includes the farm activities of non-farm landlords of farm property and, on a consolidated basis, the farm credit co-operatives. Farm credit co-operatives are closely connected with the productive activities rather than with the financial problems of the farmers. The inclusion of farm credit co-operatives in the farm business sector may therefore be justified in the US. In contrast to the treatment of farm credit co-operatives, farm marketing, purchasing, and utility co-operatives are excluded from this sector. These, as will be seen later, are in-cluded in the non-farm non-corporate sector. Other items excluded from this sector are the non-farm business activities of farm families and most consumer transactions, with the important exception of farm housing transactions, which are included in this sector.

iii. *Non-farm Non-corporate Business.* This sector covers mainly the unincorporated enterprises of trade, construction, and professions. As indicated before, it also includes marketing, purchasing, and utility co-operatives, and similar mutual organizations engaged in production or commerce. Also included in this sector are the lessorship activities of individuals and those of the non-profit organizations serving trade and business.

The reasons for having a separate sector for unincorporated business, while unincorporated, as well as incorporated farm businesses are grouped in one sector have been explained as follows by Ralph A. Young, director of the research and statistics division of the federal reserve system. 'A distinction between unincorporated and incorporated business is adhered to on institutional grounds, because the legal form of organization affects the financial patterns of business and access to financial markets, and the financial patterns and decision making of the farm business are unique to that activity, so that incorporated and unincorporated farms are grouped together in a special farm business sector.' [62, p. 329].

Because of the aims of the system, this non-farm non-corporate business sector does not include investment and commodity exchange brokers and dealers, finance companies, mortgage companies, mutual financial institutions etc., all of which are included in the appropriate financial sectors.

iv. *Corporate Business.* Included in this sector are all those private non-financial non-farm corporations which are engaged mainly in the producing and selling of goods and services. It also includes, on a consolidated basis, holding companies and closed-end investment companies. Following the groupings in the US national accounts, the flow of funds system excludes public enterprises from this sector and includes them in the Federal Government sector. It has been stated before that such sectoring in the US national accounts can only be justified on the ground that these enterprises do not constitute a relatively important part of US production. Public enterprises are usually financed on different terms from private corporations. This, for most countries, is another reason for the view expressed concerning the national accounts system that the activities of public enterprises should be shown separately.

Another sector of corporate business is formed by co-operatives, which again play a relatively unimportant part in the US economy.

However in those countries where the co-operative movement constitutes an important part of their economic structure, it would be advisable to include a separate sector for them in financial transactions accounts. The financing of co-operatives is different than that of corporations. It is particularly different for long term liabilities, which include members' shares in the co-operatives.

It would also be of great value in financial analysis to have the corporate business – in the US as well as in all other industrially developed countries – subdivided into corporations whose stock and debentures are quoted on the stock exchange and corporation whose stock is not quoted.

v. *Federal Government*. With certain exceptions, the sector includes the legislative, judicial, and executive branches of the federal government as well as all its departments and independent agencies, including all trust funds, deposit funds, and the postal savings system. (It is of interest to note that the postal savings system was originally included in the commercial banking system.) On the other hand, the sector excludes the exchange stabilisation fund, the federal reserve system, and certain monetary accounts. These are included in the commercial banking sector. Included in the government sector are also government corporations whether wholly or partly owned by government, government business-type enterprises, credit agencies, and other enterprise funds.

vi. *State and Local Government*. Included here are all the state and political sub-divisions – state government, municipalities and county councils, school districts, townships, and special districts. It also comprises the district of Columbia (excluded from the federal government sector), and the governments of territories and possessions. All the departments, trust and sinking funds, corporations, enterprises, and authorities of these governmental units are also included here.

vii. *Commercial Banking and Monetary Authorities*. One of the main objectives of the flow of funds system is to provide a statistical framework for the analysis of the relationships between financial and non-financial sectors. The system groups in this sector the monetary authorities of the economy that bear liability for the money in circulation. This is a crucial decision. Financial activity can be divided into two major parts. There is the part of the activity that helps an exchange economy to perform its operations smoothly. This is the part in which financial institutions act as reservoirs for channelling money and credits from one transactor to another. It also shifts what could be called 'free' (unenforced) savings from savers to investors and/or dissavers. The other part consists of fiscal activity, national debt, and the control of the economy through monetary regulations. This is the part of the activity by which 'forced' savings are imposed.

In view of the above differences it is not wholly obvious that a central bank – the federal reserve system in the case of the U.S. – should be included among the commercial banks of the country. On the one hand it should be admitted that the commercial banks 'co-operate' (through liquidity ratios regulations, interest rates, etc.) with the central bank in the implementing of monetary policy, and on these grounds they should be classified together. But, on the other hand, we must also remember that the central bank is a direct tool in the hands of the central government. It is through the central bank that the government carries out its monetary and economic policy. These would all be good grounds for having the central bank grouped together with the central government.

The sector includes the domestic commercial banks (excluding those in the territories and possessions), the banks of the federal reserve system and the treasury monetary funds. The mutual savings banks were also included in this sector up to 1955, but with the growing desire of the federal reserve system to show saving and investment estimates distinctly these banks now comprise a main component of a separate sector.

The assets of this sector are mainly the loan portfolio, gold and other monetary reserves, while its liabilities consist of its obligations for the currency in circulation and the bank deposits of the other sectors.

Loans, monetary reserves, deposits and other claims between the components of the commercial banking and monetary authorities sector are eliminated by consolidation. It should, however, be pointed out that the federal reserve system prepares sub-sector accounts for (a) commercial banks and (b) federal reserve and treasury monetary funds. But contrary to its original practice, these accounts are only privately circulated. In these sub-sector accounts the inter-sub-sector financial relations are traceable. It should finally be added that each sub-sector account is also constructed on a consolidated basis.

viii. *Saving Institutions.* As noted earlier, this sector was originally a sub-sector of the 'banking' sector, which was split into (a) the commercial banking and monetary authorities and (b) saving institutions, which previously also included the postal savings system. The mutual savings bank, savings and loan associations, and credit unions are now comprised in this sector. The federal reserve system prepares a sub-sector account for each of these groups but does not publish them in its bulletin.

ix. *Insurance.* In Copeland's 'Study of Moneyflows' two separate sectors were set up for insurance. In one sector all private stock and mutual life insurance companies were grouped, while the other sector consisted of 'Other Insurance Carriers' which included life and other insurance funds of fraternal orders, self-administered pension funds of incorporated and unincorporated enterprises and, finally, all other insurance such as fire, accident, casualty, marine, etc.

The federal reserve system has formally set up one insurance sector for all insurance activities but has in fact sub-divided it into three sub-sectors, viz: (a) life insurance, (b) self administered pension plans, (c) other insurance activities. Originally the federal reserve system published separate accounts for each of these sub-sectors – a practice which has recently been abandoned though the appropriate data are still prepared. It should be noted that government insurance and retirement programmes are not included in this sector. They are included with the government units sponsoring these programmes.

x. *Finance n.e.c.* Originally the flow of funds system contained a sector named 'Other Investors' which consisted of the following three sub-sectors: (a) non-profit organizations, (b) savings and loan associations, (c) financial institutions n.e.c. The saving and loan associations were combined with the savings banks and credit unions because of the desire to have all the savings institutions in a separate and special sector. The present finance n.e.c. sector consists then of sales finance companies, mortgage companies, open-end investment companies, and security and commodity exchange brokers and dealers. Banks in territories and possessions and agencies of foreign banks, excluded from the commercial banking and monetary authorities sector, are also included in this sector.

xi. *Rest of the World.* Contained in this sector are residents and governments of all countries outside the United States and its territories and possessions. It also includes all the international organizations and their foreign staff, and all the foreign embassies and consulates and their non-United States citizens employees. The foreign subsidiaries and branches of American corporations are also included in this sector as are American citizens permanently residing abroad. American subsidiaries and branches of foreign corporations as well as foreigners temporarily engaged in the United States are excluded from this sector and included in the other appropriate domestic sectors.

It will be observed from the above analysis of the structure of the ten domestic sectors and the rest of the world account that a serious endeavour has been made to sectorize the economy into its most significant decision-making units in the sphere of financial transactions. Some further breakdown of some of the sectors in the supporting tables makes the sectorizing still more refined. It remains, however, only a breakdown of the three traditional sectors of the national accounts system. The major sector added is that of the financial intermediaries which play no important role in the analytical framework of the national accounts. In some of the sectors of the flow of funds system decision-making units are included whose impact upon financial activity is different from that of the sectors in which they are included. Several important financial bodies such as the postal savings system, federal land banks, federal home loan banks, and trust funds are included in the federal government sector. In the farm business sector are also included national farm loan associations and production credit associations. Holding companies constitute part of the corporate business sector. These examples were not cited to indicate that the sectors require still further sub-divisions. With further detailed data and with the help of electronic accounting technique a still more detailed sub-division could probably be accomplished. However, the whole approach to the problem of sectoring for financial transactions accounts ought, surely, to be basically different from that for the national accounts or for the input-output system. There is in particular no justification for leaving the household sector and the corporate business sector as they now stand.

In conclusion it should be stated that the approach adopted in the U.S. flow of funds system cannot be followed universally. This is unavoidably so because the sectoring for financial transactions has to be designed largely on an institutional basis. The institutional structure and the method of operation of these institutions differ from one country to another. Sectoring would consequently have to be made on the basis of the institutional structure of the country concerned.

IV · TRANSACTION CATEGORIES IN THE UNITED STATES FLOW OF FUNDS SYSTEM

It will be convenient to begin the analysis of the transaction categories of the flow of funds system by referring to the summary of flow of funds accounts which is a 'Sector by transaction' matrix of the savings, tangible capital investments, and financial flows for the entire economy. Such a summary can be found in [58].

Detailed flows for item 'A' – gross savings – in the above summary table are given in supporting statements of sources and uses of funds for each sector of the system. It will suffice for present purposes to show the details for one of the sectors, say, the consumers and non-profit organisations sector. The details given are:

(a) Current receipts.
(b) Income receipts.
(c) Transfer receipts.
(d) Income taxes and other deductions.
(e) Taxes less tax refunds.
(f) Pensions and OASI deductions.
(g) Current receipts after deductions $(a-d)$.
(h) Current expenditure for goods and services.
(i) Net Life Insurance premiums.
(j) Current surplus $(g-h-i)$.
(k) Insurance and retirements credits.
(l) Capital consumption.
(m) Net savings $(j-k-l)$.
(n) Gross savings $(l-m)$.

Income receipts item (b) consists of wages, interest dividends, and income withdrawals from unincorporated business. Since it is the monetary flow aspect of these transactions that is of primary interest, the flow of funds system, unlike most of the national accounts systems, does not include any imputed incomes or incomes in kind in its estimates of the above income.

Item (c) – transfer receipts – records grants and donations, net of transfers within the sector, social insurance benefits, and benefits from private pension funds and government retirement funds.

Item (f) – pension and OASI deductions – consists mainly of the contributions of employees to old age and survivors insurance (OASI) and to private pension and government retirement funds.

Insurance and retirement credits – item (k) – is connected with a rather major exception to the principle of imputations introduced by the federal reserve system since August, 1959. The procedure adopted is in principle similar to a recommendation made by the conference of European statisticians at its session held in Geneva in February, 1959 [47, Annex].

Premiums paid to and benefits received from life insurance and private and government pension funds can be regarded both as current and as capital transactions. Premiums may be regarded as financial flows representing increased claims on insurance and pension funds, while the benefits can be viewed as the liquidation of such claims. It is because of the fact that these transactions are of a current as well as of a capital nature that the imputation is made in the new version of the flow of funds system.

The procedure adopted for the above imputation is that after the premiums paid and benefits received are recorded in the appropriate current transactions accounts, and after the investment incomes are added, and the operating expenses deducted, the net accrual of equity in insurance and pension funds is imputed as a current flow from these funds to consumers. Against these imputed credits, the consumers are debited (and insurance and pension funds credited) with financial investments in the transaction categories of 'Saving through Life Insurance' and 'Saving through Pension Funds'.

Item (b) in the summary – capital consumption – is a deviation from the basic purposes of the system as originally envisaged. The aim of the system was originally to measure in current money units the transactions in the current product and in existing financial and non-financial assets carried out in cash and against credit. The original system had consequently no use for 'book-keeping' transactions such as depreciation. It is, furthermore, of interest to point out here that the capital consumption estimates for non-farm capital goods are the same estimates as are used in the U.S. national accounts. It may be recalled that these estimates are computed on a straight line basis. The shortcomings of this basis for the computation of provisions for capital consumption for national accounts purposes have already been remarked upon. It was claimed that the SNA recommendation for estimating capital consumption on a replacement basis is the only consistent method for a national account system. However, if capital consumption is also to be shown in a financial transactions account it should be shown in accordance with the provisions made in the books of the enterprises. The provisions and reserves for the depreciation of the fixed assets as recorded in the accounts of the enterprises reflects the financial policies of the enterprises considerably, and their financial status even more. In addition to recording capital consumption in this way, financial transactions accounts might also show capital gains and losses (which surely ought to be shown in such accounts and which the flow of funds system systematically avoids). A more complete picture would thus be obtained for monetary policy makings and analysis.

As can be seen in the summary, the flow of funds system includes 'consumer durable goods' amongst the capital expenditure – a fact which will be remarked upon later. However, it should be remarked here that the provisions for the consumption of 'consumer durable goods' are computed on a replacement basis. The provisions for the consumption of farm capital goods are also on a replacement basis which follows the U.S. national accounts method for computing farm capital consumption. Here, as in many other matters, there is the tendency to adapt the system to the national accounts, and not to the specific aims of financial transaction accounts.

The data for capital consumption were introduced with the 1959 revision. The data are merely given as additional information and do not constitute part of the accounting framework, where gross saving and gross investment are the essential data.

Detailed data are provided in the supporting tables on saving and investment for capital consumption by consumers and non-profit organizations, farms, non-corporate and corporate – non-financial business sectors. The data for the consumers and non-profit organizations sector is further sub-divided into depreciation of consumers' durable goods, owner-occupied houses, and plant and equipment of non-profit organizations.

Gross investments: It will be noticed that the largest gross investments are those of the consumer and non-profit sector. Both the net capital expenditure and the net financial investments of this sector greatly exceed the corresponding investments of the other sectors. There is no need to comment here upon the matter of capital investments because this is essentially not the main concern of the flow of funds system. But attention should be drawn to the fact that the largest part of the financial investments made are attributed to a sector which includes a very large percentage of 'transactors' who certainly did not make and do not own these investments. This is a further reflection upon the sectorizing method of the flow of funds. Investments in the government sector are, in fact, equal to the financial investments. The flow of funds system at present shows all government expenditures as current transactions thus following the US national accounts method. Government construction expenditures are, however, separately recorded among the current transactions as shown in a supporting statement for the government sector.

It should be pointed out that the gross investments are 'gross' in the sense that they are gross of capital consumption. They are, on the other hand, net of sales of capital assets, and net of some financial assets and claims. The following two paragraphs from [57, p. 832] describe how and to what extent the financial flows are netted out.

Financial flows for each sector are recorded on a net transaction basis for each financial transaction category; that is, for each sector for each financial transaction category the asset entry represents funds used to acquire assets of that type in the accounting period less funds realized from the disposition of assets of that type in the accounting period; and the liability entry represents funds raised by borrowing less funds used in repayment in the accounting period (To simplify terminology and table form, the term 'liability' is used to cover both equity and debt claims).

In two respects, however, entries for financial flows are on a gross basis; (1) liabilities (assets) of one transaction category are not netted against assets (liabilities) of another. For example, consumer borrowing to purchase securities is not netted against consumer purchase of the securities; both are shown in the consumer account. (2) For any sector, asset and liability entries within a single transaction category are not netted; both are shown (except for internal holdings in consolidated sector accounts). For example, consumer mortgage assets are not netted against consumer mortgage liabilities.

The above netting is mainly due to a lack of gross data, and in some instances, to lack of adequate and consistent information for making the sectoral distribution. More grossing would undoubtedly improve the data for the purposes of financial and economic analysis. The gross amounts of the various loans – gross issues of loans and gross repayments – gross amounts of deposits made and withdrawn by each sector, and other gross flows could serve as important indicators of the volume and level of financial and economic activity.

Item (f) – consumer durable goods – is shown only for the consumer sector. It consists of the acquisition of houses for the occupancy of the owners, and also the purchase of other new and existing assets net of sale of existing goods. The purchases and sales of existing goods within the domestic sectors counterbalance each other and do not, consequently, add to tangible national investment. They do, however, have their impact upon the financial flows between these sectors.

There are no special comments to be made here in connexion with item (n) – plant and equipment, and item (i) – changes in inventories. These flows originate in production. They raise the problem of capital gains and losses.

It was indicated in the section on the national accounts systems that capital gains and losses, realized and unrealized, are excluded from national accounts on the grounds that they do not originate in production and cannot consequently be included in a framework designed to reflect production. This argument, which is valid for the national accounts system, cannot be used for a system of accounts which is designed to show financial transactions; certainly not in so far as realized capital gains and losses are concerned. Realized capital gains and losses put additional funds, or reduce the funds, in the hands of transactors. Such changes undoubtedly have a significant impact upon the decision-making units of the economy and bring about important redistributions of financial assets and liabilities between the various sectors of the economy.

It was suggested that there should be a record of capital gains and losses only by way of a note to domestic capital formation in the national accounts. In a financial transactions system the full incorporation of realized capital gains and losses would seem advisable, while unrealized capital gains and losses should also be recorded only by way of a note to the investments flow.

Some of the financial transaction categories will be analysed in the following sub-section. The flow aspect as well as the balances of the transactions will be considered.

V · STRUCTURE OF FINANCIAL ASSETS AND LIABILITIES IN THE US FLOW OF FUNDS SYSTEM

There are four main criteria for classifying the financial transactions in a manner relevant for financial analysis. The first criterion is liquidity. Financial transactions in short term claims have a different impact on activity in the economy from transactions in long term claims. The second criterion is risk. It is important to follow the trend of financial investors' choice with regard to the risk involved in investments on the one hand, and the type of transactors seeking for the funds saved on the other hand. It would consequently be of interest to have a relevant grouping of the seekers of funds. Such a grouping cannot be limited to government and to corporate enterprizes. A much more meaningful classification must be made. The third criterion is the legal nature of the financial instrument. Trade credit should be distinguished from consumer credit, while farm mortgages must not be shown together with mortgages on city housing. The transactions in these various categories reflect different aspects of economic and financial activity. The fourth criterion is yield. This is perhaps common to the other criteria, but there are still some transactions in which yield might be an independent consideration, particularly if importance is attached to yield in local as compared with foreign currency.

A comparison of the above criteria with those adopted by the flow of funds system will show that the list and classification of the financial transaction categories in the flow of funds system is quite exhaustive. Further improvement in the list and classification of transaction categories is to a great extent connected with the sectoring problem. A more solid and distinct sectoring for financial purposes would throw more light on the type of instruments held or owed by the sector.

It should be pointed out here that a number of changes in the financial transaction categories in the flow of funds system have been introduced since 1959. The breakdown of the deposits into demand and time deposits, the greater details for mortgage loans, the sharper division between the readily redeemable instruments against other less liquid and shiftable securities and credits are all great advantages in financial analysis.

An exceptional and significant change in the new version of the flow of funds system is the information on the financial status at the end of each year of the various sectors. Though by name the system is to show only transactions of *flows* and *changes* in financial assets and liabilities, a critical step has been made towards a link with another social accounting system, aiming to show the balance sheet of a nation.

The link is made by a simple combination, using the same sectors and the same transaction categories. Sectoring for stock aggregates should be based on criteria different from those for flow aggregates. It should be suitable for all assets – financial as well as non-financial – tangible as well as intangible.

The financial balance sheet of the US flow of funds system is in fact incomplete. For reasons given later, not all the liabilities are shown against the recorded financial assets.

In no other case where 'flow of funds' systems have been introduced in practice or recommended by experts for actual use, has such a financial balance sheet been introduced or recommended for use.

The structure of financial assets and liabilities as at the end of 1960 for each sector and for all sectors of the U.S. economy can be found in [59, p. 993]. The financial assets and liabilities shown are only those for which the flows during the period are provided.

It will be observed that the first transaction category – gold and
o

treasury currency – is divided into two separate sub-categories. The gold sub-category consists only of the gold held as a monetary reserve. The difference in the uses of funds between the commercial banking sector and the rest of the world sector is explained by the fact that the former consists of net increases and monetary gold stock plus the active gold of the exchange stabilization fund, while the latter consists of gold transactions with the United States.

It will be noted that there is no liability for the gold assets held. Though considered here as a financial asset it is nevertheless treated, in fact, as a non-financial asset. This is, incidentally, one of the relatively minor reasons for the difference between the totals of the assets and liabilities of individual sectors and of the economy as a whole.

The treasury currency transactions sub-category consists of the silver held as monetary reserve and of accounts in connexion with the minor coins, seigniorage, notes not backed by gold reserves, and in connexion with other asset-debt relationships between the banking system and the federal government.

The demand deposits and currency transaction category consists mainly of demand deposits held by all sectors with the commercial banks. It also covers government and foreign deposits with the federal reserve banks, and United States currency.

Differences in flows and in balances between all sectors and the commercial banking sector is due mainly to 'mail float' and 'bank float' – the former referring to cheques in mail transit between drawers and drawees, and the latter to cheques in the process of being cleared between banks.

The fixed value redeemable claims transaction category as well as its sub-categories are all adjusted in such a manner that the uses of funds for all sectors are equal to the sources of funds of all sectors, and the assets are equal to the liabilities. The time deposits are those held with the commercial banks, mutual savings banks which are part of the savings institutions sector, and the postal savings system which is one of the components of the federal government sector. It is these three sectors which show the sources in the flow transactions (and the liabilities in the outstanding balances) against the corresponding uses of funds (and assets) of all other sectors.

It should be remarked here that the assortment of liquidity reserves kept by commercial banks against demand and time deposits held with them is not quite suitable for determining reserve liquidity ratios. There ought to be a clearer distinction between financial instruments of primary reserve status and those of secondary reserve status. Such a differentiation would indeed lead to a still wider assortment of financial instruments according to the criteria of risk and legal status.

While it has perhaps not been of special interest for the US, it is quite important for other countries to distinguish between local and foreign deposits. The liquidity reserves to be kept against such deposits are different because of the uncertainty in the time of recalling of such deposits and because of the reserves in foreign currency which have to be kept against them.

The saving shares are with the saving and loan association and credit unions, both of which are in the savings institutions sector.

Only the savings bonds held by the consumers' sector are recorded in this transaction category. Savings bonds held by the other sectors are recorded in the federal obligations sub-category of the credit and equity market instruments category.

Savings through life insurance and pension funds' transaction categories have already been discussed while analyzing non-financial transactions. These are the financial reserves against the life insurance policies or pension plans of life insurance companies and of railroad and government employees retirement funds. The transactions are consequently recorded as a source of funds and as liabilities in the insurance sector, and in the two government sectors. The uses of funds and the assets are attributed to the consumer sector only, though some business enterprises may be beneficiaries of life insurance policies. The term 'saving' in this context is rather confusing, and as Professor Powelson has justly remarked 'is not appropriately applied to this item, which consists of a financial asset of the consumer sector whose internal contra entry is reflected in the data for

Line A, gross saving. Like currency and deposits and other financial items, the capital element of life insurance policies is the financial counterpart of saving, but is not itself saving' [31, p. 302].

It should be noted that loans obtained by policy holders from insurance companies and from the insurance programme of government sectors are not 'netted' against these reserves. These borrowings appear in the 'other loans' transaction category.

The credit and equity market instruments transaction category is sub-divided into ten sub-categories. Quantitatively, it comprises the largest part of the flows of financial transaction as well as in its outstanding balances. It is also mainly due to the non-availability of sufficient data for one of its sub-categories (corporate stock) that there is no equality between the outstanding balances of assets and liabilities of the individual sectors, and of the totals for all sectors. What characterizes most of the items in this category is that they are of long term duration. Some indications as to the distribution of these instruments according to dates of repayment would be an important contribution to financial analysis.

Included in the federal obligations transaction sub-category are mainly saving bonds held by non-consumers, and treasury bills. Some of the supporting statements for the individual sectors provide data about the distribution into short term, guaranteed and non-guaranteed obligations.

Recorded in the state and local obligations sub-category are all debts, except loans from the federal government, and trade debts of all state and local government units. The recording is gross in the sense that the holdings of the obligations of one state or local government unit by another state or local government unit are not netted out one against another.

The corporate and foreign bonds sub-category covers the bonded debt of private corporations in the USA and private, governmental, and international agency bonds of foreign countries.

Flows in the corporate stock sub-category show net issues, purchases and sales of all domestic corporate stock, and net purchases of stock of foreign corporations. The uses and sources of all sectors balance out one against another. In the structure of financial assets and liabilities, on the other hand, there is no balance. The indication with regard to the fact that no liabilities are shown against the issued corporate stock is that data are 'not available'. The reasons for the non-availability of such important data are twofold. One reason is that stock cannot in a practical sense be considered as a liability of a corporation, the 'debtor'. It is only because of the legal and double entry accountancy concepts, that a corporation is viewed as a separate entity and consequently can be indebted to the stockholders – the 'outsiders'. This is more or less a technical reason. This reason has already been pointed out in our examples illustrating the contrasts between the flow of funds system and the national accounts system. The second reason lies in the fact that to evaluate the outstanding corporate stock would in practice mean evaluating the tangible and intangible assets of the corporation. It would also mean introducing the estimation of capital gains and losses. With all these additions on the assets side, the corporate stock on the liabilities side would have to be shown in two parts: one part showing the par value or the value at which it was sold by the issuing corporation; the second part would have to show the increase or decrease of the assets which it represents. This would certainly involve making additional estimates of a complicated nature. Such a task might, however, well be regarded as one appropriate to a financial flow system. As previously indicated, it is mainly because of the omission of data on the liabilities for the corporate stock that the total of all assets held by all sectors differs markedly from the total of all liabilities of all sectors.

Mortgages – (z) and (a) – are not only not readily redeemable, but are also not easily transferable. The data given in the flow of funds system provides satisfactory information for the analysis as to type and sectoral distribution.

Included in the consumer credit transaction sub-category are short term and intermediate term credits, on either an instalment or a non-instalment basis. These consist of both bank and non-bank credit.

Security credit covers credit granted by security brokers and dealers and loans issued by banks for the purchase or holding of securities.

Bank loans consist of commercial and industrial loans, agricultural loans, loans to individuals, other loans to various institutions, and loans to foreign banks. These loans are all handled by the commercial banking sector. Loans by one domestic bank to another are eliminated by consolidation of the banking sector statement.

Other loans, n.e.c. consist of finance company and other open market paper, bankers acceptances, loans by the federal government (quantitatively the largest part), loans by finance companies to business, loans by mutual savings banks and, as indicated in the analysis of transaction categories (s) and (t), loans on life insurance policies.

The trade credit transaction category consists of accounts and notes receivable and payable.

The proprietors' net investment in non-corporate business, (g) transaction category, appears only in the summary of flow of funds, because it is only the net flow of equity funds invested by proprietors in unincorporated farm and non-farm business that is shown. No outstanding balances are estimated for the structure of financial assets and liabilities. There are difficulties – statistical and conceptual – in ascertaining the investments by proprietors of unincorporated business. The method adopted by the flow of funds system is to define these investments as being equal to the net investment expenditures by the non-corporate business in non-financial and financial assets less increases in liabilities and less allowances for capital consumption.

'Miscellaneous financial transactions instruments' cover a variety of equity items and deposits. Among these equity items are included private interest in government corporations, capital stock of the exchange stabilization fund, federal government subscriptions to international financial institutions, etc. The deposits are mainly those of the federal government with international financial institutions, of foreign banks, agencies and branches, etc. The category also includes unidentified financial assets and liabilities of the rest of the world.

VI · SOME CONCLUDING REMARKS ON THE FLOW OF FUNDS SYSTEM

The discussion of the flow of funds system has brought out a number of points which call at least for strengthening, if not for drastic change. It would seem that the system has not been theoretically hammered out to the same extent as have the other two social accounts of flow previously discussed.

The major weakness lies in the sectoring of the economy for financial transactions as well as for the structure of financial assets and liabilities. The sectoring follows, though admittedly with some further breakdown, that of the national accounts. The orientation of these two systems is basically different and this should be made obvious by the different sectoring. The sectoring of an economy is the backbone of a social accounting system. The consumer sector cannot be regarded as an institutional grouping. Consumers differ greatly in their financial behaviour and ownership. Another method of grouping households for financial accounts purposes seems imperative. Non-profit institutions should certainly not be grouped in this sector. For the same reason that farm enterprises are separated from non-farm enterprises, public enterprises and co-operatives should also be grouped separately. The financial decision-making and opportunities of such enterprises are different. Corporations should be divided according to their status at the stock exchange. The changes in sectoring should be made with an eye to strengthening the structure of financial assets and liabilities which should, in the author's opinion, have priority in development.

The classification of the transaction categories is in general very useful. The only major criticisms are:

    1. No capital gain or losses are shown. These gains or losses are of great importance in the financial and economic behaviour of the transactors and a financial accounting system. One of the reasons that the structure of the financial assets and liabilities of the flow of funds system is not brought to balance is that stock 'liabilities' with their changing market values are not shown.

2. Partly because of the shortcomings in the sectoring, as pointed out above, and partly due to the classification of the transaction categories, there is no clear and convenient way of analyzing the liquid reserves and reserve ratios kept by banks against short and long term deposits.

3. The estimates of the consumption of fixed capital for a financial accounting system should follow the actual financial provisions made by all the holders of these real assets. Unlike the national accounts system, where the provisions should indicate the real amortization of the assets and their obsolescence, a financial system should aim more at showing the financial reserves set aside for this purpose. The flow of funds system in fact follows neither one method nor the other. It simply uses the data for the national accounts of the US where this flow was critically discussed earlier in our study.

VII · NATIONAL TRANSACTIONS ACCOUNTS FOR CANADA

A. INTRODUCTORY NOTE

While the US flow of funds system can be said to be already in its third stage of development, the Canadian national transactions accounts are admittedly only a 'pioneering endeavour' [22, p. 467]. The division of research and statistics of the federal reserve system also had satisfactory statistical data available and evidently all the necessary encouragement to compile additional material to fill in the gaps disclosed in the information for the system, while the central research and development staff of the Canadian bureau of statistics were confronted with the problem of compiling adequate material. It is apparently also because of the inadequate sources of statistical data and limited resources that the national transactions accounts prepared for the years 1946–54 have not been brought up to date. An analysis of the national transactions accounts is of interest mainly because of the significant fact that though they were inspired and stimulated by the 'moneyflows' and 'flow of funds' studies, they were 'set up to complement rather than to compete with the national product accounts' [32, p. 42]. They were an attempt to combine the national accounts with the financial transactions of the country.

B. SECTORING OF THE ECONOMY

With the approach that the national transactions accounts are to be an extension of the national accounts, the sectoring of the economy takes on the form of a sub-division of the sectors for the national accounts of Canada. The sectoring for the national transactions accounts has only been somewhat expanded. The following is a comparison of the sectoring of the national accounts and the national transactions accounts of Canada.

Sectoring in the national accounts	Sectoring in the national transactions accounts
Persons	Consumers
Businesses	Unincorporated business
	Non-financial corporations
	Government enterprises
	Banking
	Life insurance
	Other finance
Governments	Federal government
	Provincial governments
	Municipal governments
Non-residents	Rest of the world

The consumer sector is mainly limited to households in their transactions as consumers. Transactions which have a clear business character have been excluded from the persons sector and included in the unincorporated business sector. As in the US flow of funds system, the national transactions accounts also exclude from the consumers sector the lessorship activities of households in their capacity as houseowners. In the flow of funds system these transactions are allocated between the farm sector and the non-corporate non-financial business sector, whereas the national transactions accounts, having no separate farm sector, include transactions in the unincorporated business sector. Self-administered or pension funds and other forms of private trust funds, and non-profit institutions, have been included in this sector. The consumer's sector in this system as well as in all other financial transaction systems is probably the least satisfactorily constituted. One of the basic principles in sectoring for a financial transactions system is that the transactors should be classified according to their ownership of financial assets. To include all consumers into one sector makes this sector meaningless. The inclusion of pension funds in this sector is an additional shortcoming. The sector becomes thereby practically similar to a household sector in the national accounts where the sectoring is mainly on a functional basis.

The unincorporated business sector consists of all unincorporated trade and enterprise and professional practitioners. Unlike the flow of funds system, the national transaction accounts do not have a separate sector for farming and this is consequently also included in this sector. The components of this sector are in effect very similar to those of a sub-sector of the enterprise sector of a national accounts system.

Included in the non-financial corporations sector are all non-financial corporations and co-operatives. The fact that the sector also includes public corporations is a definite shortcoming. The current as well as the long term financing of public corporations is significantly different from the financing of private corporations. In rather conspicuous contrast to the United States flow of funds system, the sector also includes some financial enterprises, such as stock, bond, and commodity brokers and dealers. It also includes the unincorporated branches of foreign corporations and the Canadian operations of foreign owned corporations.

The government enterprises sector includes enterprises owned and operated by the government and performing the activities of similar enterprises in the non-financial corporations sector. Internally the sector is subdivided into: (a) federal enterprises, (b) provincial and municipal enterprises, and (c) operation of government buildings. The last subsector is connected with the treatment of government buildings in the Canadian national accounts. According to this treatment, government buildings are considered to be operated by a business agency which receives gross rent from government and pays back net rent which is the gross rent less amounts set aside for capital consumption. It will be remembered that in the flow of funds system government enterprises are included in the government sector. In the United States these do not constitute an important part of the economy's activity, and are in principle not regarded there as enterprises in the ordinary sense. Such an approach cannot always be shared by other countries, particularly where government enterprises constitute an important part of the country's activity.

The banking sector includes all the chartered banks, the bank of Canada, and the exchange fund. The structure of this sector is similar to that of the commercial banking and monetary authorities sector in the flow of funds system. It is of interest to note that Canadian experience has shown that the inclusion of the exchange fund, which contains most of the foreign short term assets, is liable to cause distortion in the overall pricture of the banking sector as a whole. This is due to the fact that foreign short term assets are exposed to rather wide variations. The US flow of funds system, as indicated before, includes the exchange stabilization fund in the federal government sector, and not in the commercial banking sector.

The life insurance sector consists of Canadian companies operating under federal registration, provincially licensed companies and Canadian transactions of British and foreign companies. Unlike the flow of funds system, the national transactions accounts do not include all insurance activities – life and non-life – in one sector. The non-life insurance companies comprise part of the following sector.

The 'other finance' sector includes a wide range of financial institutions. It consists of thirteen groups as listed in [22, p. 541].

A comparison of these groups with the sectoring of the flow of funds system indicates that in the latter system these groups would be included in four different sectors – three of which would be within the financial sectors while one would be in the government sector.

A conglomeration of all the above institutions into one sector might indeed have been due to technical difficulties. No doubt more statistical data and more experience of their arrangement are required.

The national transactions accounts have a separate sector for the provincial governments and a separate sector for the municipal governments as compared with only one sector – state and local governments – in the flow of funds system.

C. TRANSACTION CATEGORIES

A summary of the national transactions accounts for 1954 can be found in [22]. As pointed out in the introductory note, this is the last year for which the national transactions accounts were prepared.

Transaction categories in the systems are divided into three parts, viz: (1) current transactions account (A account), (2) investment transactions account (B account), and (3) financial transactions account and other transactions and errors (C and D accounts). The system provides data for transactions of flow only. The following statement is of interest in connexion with this limitation:

We may also hope that the future developments will give us 'stock' data comparable with the 'flows' data contained in the B and C accounts. To interpret certain flows, an assessment of the base to which they add or from which they subtract is essential [32, p. 54].

As indicated earlier, a change from 'flow' to 'stock' data would require a basic change in sectoring. It has also been observed in the analysis of the structure of the financial assets and liabilities given in the flow of funds system that the evaluation of at least some of the financial obligations entails in fact an evaluation of the tangible and non-tangible assets and capital gains and losses which the financial instruments represent.

VIII · FRENCH NATIONAL ACCOUNTS – FINANCIAL PART RESTATED

A. SECTORING FOR FINANCIAL PURPOSES

When examining the sectoring of the economy according to the

French national accounts system it was shown that the simplified accounts provide a separate sector for financial intermediaries. This in itself, apart from the other differences in the transactors included in each sector, is different from most of the national accounts systems where the financial intermediaries constitute part of the enterprise sector. The expanded accounts contain data on financial transactions of all sectors in addition to the economic transactions commonly shown by the national accounts systems. In other words they start out from the capital account of their national accounts (Tableau économique) with the presentation of the changes in financial assets and liabilities. This procedure is different from that of the US flow of funds system or the national transactions accounts for Canada where the financial transactions accounts start out with the income accounts. It is then only for the capital account that the expanded accounts sub-divide the financial institutions sector into three separate sectors, viz: (a) the banking system, (b) other financial institutions, (c) the treasury (state).

The banking system sector consists of the commercial banks, the Banque de France, and the exchange stabilization funds. The sector does not include the agricultural credit banks. These are included in the other financial institutions.

Included in the other financial institutions sector are (a) all specialized credit institutions such as savings and loans associations, agricultural banks, intermediate term credit funds, instalment credit and marketing credit establishments, and (b) all insurance companies.

It will be recalled that in the simplified system the treasury (state) is part of the administration sector. In the expanded system, however, the treasury constitutes a separate sector. Included in this sector are special trust and sinking funds, domestic and overseas social and economic development investment funds, and the issue of currency and coinage.

The sectoring in the expanded accounts in fact adds no more than two sectors of financial institutions to the national accounts as commonly in use in other western countries. It is not so much the number of sectors as the specific and distinct sectoring that is relevant for financial analysis. By adding these two financial sectors to the other sectors which are constituted on a functional basis, the financial data add very little towards visualizing the interdependence between the productive and the financial activity of an economy. The financial data made available in this combined system is but a limited subdivision of the financial aggregates given in financial statistics. This is not the central aim of a social accounting system.

B. FINANCIAL TRANSACTION CATEGORIES

Not only is the number of sectors in the French expanded system less than in the other financial systems (eight in the French system as compared with eleven in the United States flow of funds system and the Canadian national transaction accounts), but also the number of financial transaction categories is limited to ten as compared with twenty in the flow of funds system and seventeen in the national transactions accounts. In this section the main criteria for listing and grouping financial transaction categories have been outlined. The number and grouping of financial transactions categories in the expanded accounts do not, as will be observed, fully meet these requirements. Too many financial transactions are combined into one category. There is consequently little indication as to the differences in risk, or in legal form, or in repayment periods of the financial instruments for which the changes are shown. A summary of financial transactions for 1960 is given in [18, p. 972].

The money transaction category consists of the money issued by the Banque de France – bank notes and deposits, current deposits and checking accounts in banks, 'sundry creditors' as a result of 'advances' granted, and 'sundry debtors' accounts. It also includes money issued by the treasury and deposits with the treasury and other financial institutions.

Included in the 'other deposits' category are fixed term deposits with banks and agricultural credit institutions, deposits with saving banks, deposits with the treasury in connexion with special accounts, and sundry deposits with specialized credit establishments.

The 'short term bills' transaction category consists mainly of credits for less than five years. It also includes treasury bills, three to five years bonds of agricultural credit institutions, and other short term bonds of reconstruction funds of the treasury.

The debentures transaction consist of all long term debentures of public and private corporations – domestic, overseas or foreign. It should be noted here that the gross flow is recorded for this category. Collections and repayments are shown in the accounts separately. By deducting these collections and repayments the net changes in assets and liabilities can be computed.

In the shares category are grouped the shares and stocks of all registered companies – domestic as well as foreign.

Short term credits consist of credits for less than two years, and mainly of commercial credits for a duration of three months. The credits are those granted by banks in the form of discount credits to enterprises, as consumers' credits, and as short term advances to treasury and to other administrative entities included in the administration sector. They also include short term credit facilities to overseas territories and foreign countries.

Intermediate term credits consist of: (a) credits granted by banks to enterprises as discount credit renewable during several years, which can be re-discounted at certain financial institutions and at the Banque de France, (b) financial instruments, renewable within five years, issued by mortgage credit companies to other financial institutions as security for building loans. These instruments can also be rediscounted at other financial institutions and at the Banque de France.

Included in the 'long term loans' transaction category are loans to enterprises, to administrative bodies, to the treasury, and to overseas territories and the rest of the world. Such loans are issued by the treasury for construction and development purposes, by the mortgage credit and agricultural institutions, and by similar special financial institutions. The category includes the private long term investments of the category of the rest of the world in France, and French investments abroad. The estimates of the transaction flows are given on a gross basis. Amounts collected and repaid are separately recorded. Deducting these collections or repayments, the net changes in assets and liabilities are obtained.

The gold and foreign exchange and foreign exchange obligations of the banking system are divided into two parts: (a) gold and foreign exchange with the Banque de France and the exchange stabilization funds, and gold and foreign exchange kept by the banks, (b) foreign exchange obligations of the Banque de France and the exchange stabilization funds to foreign and international financial institutions, and obligations of the banks to their foreign correspondents.

The 'intermediaries notes, deposits, and advances' transaction category can also be divided into two parts: (a) obligations of the banking system which consist of the current accounts of the treasury with the Banque de France and other funds deposited by the treasury with the Banque de France, (b) obligations of the treasury which consist of obligations against advances of the Banque de France to the treasury, treasury notes with financial institutions and deposits of financial institutions with the treasury.

CHAPTER FIVE

Integration of the Social Accounting Systems

I · STRUCTURES AND SUPERSTRUCTURES

None of the economists and statisticians who first conceived the structure of each of the existing social accounting systems intended to measure all the economic and financial aspects of an economy. They each made extraordinary contributions to an all inclusive and self sustained accounting framework for a major aspect of economic or financial activity in the economy within a certain period of time, or to some aspect of the financial and economic status of an economy at certain stages of its development. They were not unaware of all the other accounts and/or financial aspects which were excluded from their systems. They were, however, convinced that not only are these other aspects irrelevant to their systems, but that they would vitiate the purpose for which they were designed. These were their original convictions.

The national accounts system was originally, and must always be, mainly oriented towards the analysis of a welfare economy and towards assisting in its decision-making processes. The open model of the input-output system is an admirable tool for planning purposes and is also well suited to forecasting. Statistically it can also be regarded as a deconsolidation of the national accounts system, excluding the various transfers accounts. The main use of the flow of funds system ought to be in the field of monetary policy. These are the different orientations and uses of the social accounting systems of flow from the national point of view.

In planning the structure of the systems, there were, generally speaking, three prerequisites to fulfill. The first and most crucial prerequisite was to sector the economy for the role the system was to play in economic or financial analysis. Throughout this discussion, one of the major aims has been to show that the sectoring of all these systems leaves much to be desired. Nevertheless it should be realized that because of the great difficulties involved in obtaining statistical data, not to mention other practical difficulties, 'ideal' sectoring cannot be easily achieved in a market economy, and perhaps it cannot be achieved at all. It must also be admitted that each system has done the best it could under the circumstances towards sectoring for its own purposes. Furthermore it should be added that any conceptual change in the approach towards sectoring of any of the systems is very liable to put the whole structure of the system out of focus.

A second prerequisite, of undoubted theoretical importance, is that each system should constitute a consistent and interrelated framework for the various statistical aggregates and indices previously used (not unsuccessfully) for economic and financial analysis. Components which would be foreign to the role of these structures in theoretical analysis and in practical economic planning and policy-making were purposely avoided. The systems were designed to show the interrelationships between the components and aggregates relevant to their respective purposes. This meant that they were also capable of pointing out what data were still required to keep the structures stable, useful, and free of gaps. The third prerequisite was that the systems should in their final form be constructed in a compact set of accounts and tables. This brevity and compactness adds a great deal to the clarity of the major points brought out, and makes the system particularly convenient for practical users. It must be remembered that social accounting systems, probably more than any other statistical compilation, are used by a great number of private and public institutions, social organizations, and government authorities.

Despite these facts there has been a tendency during recent years to combine the existing accounting structures into one single super-structure. The recommendations put forward and the actual steps made do not propose a single solid, stable system. They are largely nothing but a certain technical cohesion of one system to another. They superimpose one structure upon another, creating a super-structure which may not have an application as stable, meaningful, and useful as the individual structures have, and is likely to be much less convenient to use.

The following analysis of the proposed methods of integration is restricted mainly to the systems of flow which are within the scope of this study.

II · INTEGRATING FINANCIAL TRANSACTIONS WITH NATIONAL ACCOUNTS

The inclination to integrate financial transactions with the national accounts system exists in two different groups, one of which would like to see the flow of funds system integrated with the national accounts system, and the other of which would like to have the national accounts expanded to include financial transactions accounts.

A. FLOW OF FUNDS SYSTEM AND U.S. INCOME AND OUTPUT SYSTEM

A determined initiative is shown by the division of research and statistics of the federal reserve system to have the flow of funds system integrated with the U.S. income and output system. The national income division of the office of business economics which prepares the accounts of the U.S. income and output system, on the other hand, shows no apparent interest in this integration. In 1955, about three years after the federal reserve system took over the study of moneyflows from Professor Copeland, the division of research and statistics still held strongly to the view that each social accounting system reflects a different analytic orientation and is constructed accordingly. It clearly pointed out that the focus of the flow of funds accounts in the interplay between financial and non-financial factors in the economy results in a substantially different selection and organization of economic data from those found in these other widely used systems of national accounts. The inclusion of transactions in existing assets and in financial claims, the inclusion of each sector account of all transactions in which the components of the sector engage, and the grouping of economic units so as to distinguish participants in credit as well as goods and service transactions, reflect the analytic orientation of the system, an orientation towards problems in which economic decisions are influenced by flows and stocks of financial claims as well as by current production, income, and consumption [56, p. 16].

In 1957, some inclination, albeit reserved towards the integration of the social accounting systems could already be observed in the division, as is evident from the following statement made by its director, Mr A. Young, before the sub-committee on economic statistics;

The effectuation of a Single Integrated System of Accounts must be regarded as a long-range goal and one whose exact form cannot be foretold now. In this development, we must be careful that attainment of formal integration does not hamper the operational usefulness of each of the individual systems or make too cumbersome their joint use in integrated analysis [60, p. 83].

The first efforts of the division of research and statistics of the federal reserve system were in fact devoted to a reconciliation of the figures in the flow of funds system with those of the US national income and output system. This was no more than a technical task which might have had its justification. The mere reconciliation of the figures however brought about the tendency to combine the flow of funds accounts with those of the national accounts system. The reconciliation of the figures in two social accounting systems can be justified and even encouraged as long as it is done for checking purposes. Such a reconciliation should not however be taken as being a synthesis of the concepts underlying the figures given in the different systems. A disregard for the uniqueness of the concepts of a system leads to instability in the structure of the whole accounting system, making it unfit for the analytical and decision making purposes for which it was conceived.

In the publication of the 1959 version of the flow of funds system the tendency towards this combination took on a definite and practical expression. The number of sectors and sub-sectors were increased and components of one sector were shifted to another one, all with the explicit aim of making the sectoring of the flow of funds system more similar to that of the national accounts system. The new sectoring has already been examined in the section on the flow of funds system. Further sectoring and subsectoring could probably be made, involving of course the need for a large amount of additional statistical data and all the costs connected with this. Such a step would perhaps help to improve the data for the national accounts but would contribute little to a more meaningful financial analysis. A system of financial transactions accounts must be based primarily on homogeneity in the financial behaviour of the transactors and on the financial assets they hold or the liability they owe. Such a grouping of transactors cannot coincide with the grouping for national accounts purposes unless the sectoring is overstretched.

Though some of the changes introduced in the estimation of flows, like estimating current flows on an accrual basis are desirable for the improvement of the data on financial transactions, several other changes did little except to reduce the clarity of the flow of funds system. Further vistas into the dynamics and structure of the flow of funds system could have been opened by strengthening the transaction categories. These refinements would make the flow of funds system more distinct and concrete in its aims, which cannot and should not be synthesised with the aims of the national accounts.

It has already been indicated that the flow of funds system introduced the presentation of financial balance sheets showing the structure of financial assets and liabilities at the end of each year. With this innovation the federal reserve system made an attempt towards the integration of yet another social accounting system, the national balance sheet system, which is in an early stage of development. It may well be that it is more feasible to integrate the flow of funds system with the national balance sheet system than with the social accounting systems of flow with which we are concerned here.

B. NATIONAL TRANSACTIONS ACCOUNTS AND NATIONAL ACCOUNTS OF CANADA

The initiative for recording financial transactions accounts as complementary accounts to the national accounts of Canada was also mainly due to a body outside the dominion bureau of statistics, which prepares the national accounts. The sets of accounts of the financial transactions for the years 1946–54 were part of a study of the finance of the economic activity of Canada which was encouraged by a Royal Commission on Canada's economic prospects (the Gordon commission) created in 1955.

It had been shown that the data on financial transactions in this system have been added as financial counterparts to the savings and investment balances of the national accounts. By using the balances of the national accounts, the national transactions accounts system has taken over structural arrangements from the national accounts system designed for other purposes. It has taken over all the netting used in the national accounts system, such as the netting of transactions in existing assets and the deduction of fixed capital consumption; it has taken over all the accruals used for the estimating of current flows; and it has taken over the imputed income included in the national accounts.

In the sphere of sectoring, the national transactions accounts followed institutional grouping only to the extent that the required data were available. We have seen that the business sector of the Canadian national accounts has been divided into six sectors. This sub-division may have been meaningful for the financial transactions but it certainly added sectors which are superfluous for the purposes of the national accounts.

It is understood that the dominion bureau of statistics in fact had second thoughts about continuing with the national transactions accounts as originally set up. Though this need not be interpreted as a complete rejection of the ideas on integration sponsored by the

Gordon commission, it certainly indicates that the integration of financial transactions accounts with national accounts requires a great deal of further thought and empirical research. A mere cohesion of the two systems only reduces their successful application to the purposes for which they were each designed.

It may be recalled that it is also the office of business economics, which prepares the US national accounts, that shows no enthusiasm about the integration of the flow of funds system with the national accounts.

C. THE FRENCH EXPANDED ACCOUNTS

In contrast to the above two systems where the initiative to integrate with the national accounts came from units engaged in the study and preparation of the financial transactions accounts, the French expanded accounts were the initiative of the French ministry of finance. It has already been stated that the expanded accounts which also include data on the changes in financial assets and liabilities, were prepared as a sequel to the simplified accounts, or Tableau économique. The disaggregated structure of the Tableau économique, with its detailed flows – current and capital – for each sector, must show all transfers and other financial movements between all the sectors if it is to avoid loose ends. Transfers and lendings and borrowings between all sectors could indeed also be shown in an aggregated system as, for instance, recommended by SNA. But in the latter system they would be introduced as a conceptual change in the framework, and would not affect the aggregative structure, though they would make it less fully articulated.

The only change in the sectoring in the expanded system as compared with the simplified system has been the sub-dividing of the financial institutions sector, which also constitutes one of the domestic sectors in the Tableau économique, into three parts – the treasury (taken out from the administration sector), the banking system, and the other financial institutions. The enterprise sector has been left unchanged. The sectoring is therefore practically on a general functional basis which is of limited use in financial analysis. It will suffice to mention the fact that there is no separate sector for farming, which is one of the large industries in France, and that the specialised financial institutions for corporate and non-corporate farming are included in the 'other financial institutions' sector. Financing corporate farming involves different financial problems and requires different solutions to those for, say, mineral deposits corporations. A *sine qua non* in sectoring for financial transactions is that it be constructed on an institutional basis.

The number of transaction categories is rather limited, particularly for some of the sectors. An expansion of the transaction categories would, of course, necessitate further appropriate sectoring and the compilation of more statistical data.

The additional financial information given in the expanded accounts cannot be taken as a serious attempt to provide an integrated systematic set of accounts providing both the data on production, consumption, and investments expected of a national accounts system, and the data on the various financial transactions expected of a flow of funds system. It actually hampers the development of the underlying concepts and presentation of the national accounts adopted by western countries.

D. UNITED NATIONS TENTATIVE PROPOSAL FOR THE INTEGRATION OF FINANCIAL FLOWS INTO A NATIONAL ACCOUNTS SYSTEM

By recording all current and capital transfers within the system, and also lendings and borrowings from one domestic sector to another, as well as to and from the rest of the world, SNA, as already observed, has in fact left an open door through which to enter into the financial sphere. It has already been pointed out why this open door is a shortcoming of SNA. It was also pointed out that OEEC has not made similar recommendations, and that neither the UK system nor the US system of national accounts have followed the SNA recommendations in this respect.

The statistical office of the United Nations, taking SNA as a starting point, submitted for consideration a form of accounts for the 'integration of financial flows into a system of national accounts' [45]. The study was sponsored by the statistical office, the economic commission for Latin America, and the bureau of technical assistance operations (all of the United Nations) and the inter-American statistical institute, in co-operation with the government of Brazil. The accounts recommended were constructed after an exhaustive study of the methods adopted by a number of countries to cope with the problem of interrelating the national accounts with the financial accounts. The construction of the accounts was also influenced to no small extent by the thinking of the expert group on statistics of changes in financial assets as set down in [47], and the exploratory work of the working group which was reported in [46] – both of the conference of European statisticians. Though these groups were formally confined to the study of a system for the presentation of financial transactions, they raised the question of the desirability of integrating financial accounts into an overall system of national accounts. The proposed United Nations form of accounts also incorporated, with some omissions, several recommendations made jointly by the United Nations and the international monetary fund in [51]. One of the major omissions is that of excluding the financial balance sheet from the integrated system recommended by the United States and the international monetary fund.

Though these are only proposed recommendations at a study stage, and though they have so far had no impact upon the practical work of statistical offices in the industrially developed countries, it would nevertheless be of interest to analyse this serious attempt to solve a complicated problem in social accounting.

Ten sectors, including the rest of the world sector, are recommended in the U.N. proposal for integrated accounts. It is obvious upon comparison how much of the proposed sectors have been influenced by the flow of funds system.

The accounting structure of the proposed system is a combination of the SNA basic accounts plus a financial transactions account. This means that in addition to the three basic accounts – the production account, the appropriation account, and the capital account

– of the national accounts system, all of which constitute part of the standard accounts of the integrated system, there is added a fourth, the financial transactions account. For each of the nine domestic sectors there are, then, four accounts. For the rest of the world there are only three accounts – a current account, a capital account, and a financial transactions account. The set of standard accounts opens with the three first aggregative accounts of SNA: (1) domestic product, (2) national income, (3) domestic capital formation. A fourth aggregate account is devoted to a summary of the financial transactions. The number of standard accounts add up, thus, to 43 accounts instead of the total of nine accounts in SNA.

Because of the enlarged number of sectors, the articulated presentation of some transactions also necessitates four matrices for the following four transactions items: (a) goods and services, (b) interest, (c) dividends, and (d) other financial transactions. Even if the following statement in [45, p. 24] is conceded 'that the matrices are not an integral part of the accounts but are used to illustrate the articulation of these items and to define their conceptual content', we are still left with a system comprised of 43 standard accounts which makes it rather a cumbersome document. Quite a number of accounts are not only superfluous for the analysis of productive activity, but also create an obscure picture of it. This is particularly so with regard to the production account of the households, etc., sector, the government sectors, and the financial sectors. By the same token many of the existing accounts are not directly required for financial analysis, particularly the detailed production accounts. To the extent that more production accounts are desirable, they are desirable on a different sectoring basis, e.g. the industry basis used in the input-output system.

Additional appropriation accounts would be required for a more meaningful presentation of the distribution of factor incomes. Wider or different presentation would, as indicated before, involve additional sectoring.

The additional sectors (additional with respect to the SNA sectoring) recommended in the proposed integrated system add very little significant data for production, income, consumption, and saving analysis. As to the financial analysis, it has already been remarked that a mere stretching of the existing traditional sectors of the national accounts is not a solution to the proper sectoring for a financial transactions accounts system.

The setting up of additional and doubtful sectors and the inclusion of irrelevant data for one or the other purpose is not the only sacrifice made for the sake of integrating financial transactions into the national accounts. A great sacrifice caused by the proposed integration is the curtailing of relevant data. A financial transactions accounts system should wherever and whenever statistically possible show all flows on a gross basis. The proposed integrated standard accounts, which follow the SNA structure, show only net flows. It is with the help of the supporting matrices that gross flows of payments for goods and services, interest, and dividends can be obtained. Similar matrices would have to be constructed for at least some of the major financial transactions, such as lending and borrowing, money, deposits, etc. Imputations, which in the author's opinion should be expanded to a maximum in the national accounts, are limited here to the minimum. This is of course due to the fact that imputations involve no financial transactions. This point should be stressed here because theoretically production activity need involve no financial transactions in this sense. The fact that production is expressed in money terms does not necessarily imply that there has been a financial transaction. Accruals which are significant for the national accounts are omitted. Differences in valuation, as, for instance, differences due to capital gains and losses, which would be of interest in a financial transactions system, are not accounted for. The proposed integrated system can also be criticized on the ground that the list of the financial transaction categories is rather limited. While some categories could be added without disturbing the proposed system, others would involve changes in the whole structure.

Because of the close adherence to the cash and credit flows and because of the financial institutions and the financial transaction categories characteristic of western industrially developed countries, the proposed accounts could not with any great advantage be used in developing countries.

It would be of interest to mention here how another international organization has approached the problem. The OEEC in [29] made an attempt to provide a systematic survey of the sources and uses of finance of its member countries, and also tried to indicate how one could move from the national accounts aggregates to the financial aggregates. It approached the problem with rather more originality. The financial data provided is for four sectors only. Enterprises and households are combined in one sector. The production figures are for a year previous to the financial data, and financial transaction categories are classified differently.

III · INPUT-OUTPUT AND NATIONAL ACCOUNTS SYSTEMS

In the analysis of the existing and proposed combined systems of national accounts and flow of funds, the basic differences between these two systems were pointed out, as were difficulties involved in integrating them. It was shown that desirable improvements in one of these two systems makes their integration still less possible. It was also indicated that the structure of financial institutions, the types of the financial transactions, and the transaction categories vary from one country to another.

In contrast to all these conceptual and technical differences between the national accounts system and the flow of funds system, there are many meeting points between the national accounts and the input-output tables.

The construction of the open model of the input-output system opened the way, in fact, towards a structural integration of the input-output system with that of the national accounts. Though the original motives and aims in the construction of the open model were closely connected with the mobilization of productive resources for military purposes during the Second World War, and with the reorganization of industries after the war, it immediately became evident that the model could also serve as an efficient tool for economic planning in peace time. It was soon realized that information on the expenditure on gross domestic product and the gross domestic income given in the national accounts system could be regarded as the corresponding 'final bill of goods' and 'primary inputs' of the exogenous part of the open model. In the original use of the open model the external part was given as a predetermined plan to be fulfilled, while in the later application of it (particularly in the non-planned economies) the final bill of goods and primary inputs were taken from the national accounts or their projections for a coming year. The framework of the open model is such that it can be used without variation in both cases.

There is no reason why the endogenous part of the input-output tables which show the inter-industrial flow of production should not be linked up with the value of the total consolidated production, and with the income of the factors of production that constitute the primary inputs required for the productive activity. The quantities of the 'final bill' are measured in the same units as the other inter-industrial flows of output. This is also, *mutatis mutandis*, true with regard to the 'primary inputs'. The aggregates of domestic product and expenditure of the national accounts can therefore be regarded from the point of view of quantitative accounting as an integral part of the whole production process in an economy. The integration of the national accounts with the input-output tables portrays the position. The transfers between sectors, including rest of the world, and factor income from abroad can of course have no place in such integrated accounts. An integration of the product accounts with the input-output tables, was in fact made, for instance, in the input-output tables for the United Kingdom for 1954 [38], and according to [44, p. 3] 'input-output tables have been brought within the framework of the national income accounts . . . in a number of European countries.' The open model makes this integration practically a structural necessity. By integrating the open model of the input-output system with the national accounts system, the ex-post figures of the latter system assume an additional role in the 'forecasting' possibilities of the former system.

The preparation of input-output tables even for a minimum number of 'industries' is a costly undertaking. These costs can be avoided in free market economies where there is no pressing need for annual input-output tables as long as no marked changes have taken place in the cost structure of the productive process. The position is presumably different in planned economies where the input-output tables are mostly predetermined. The preparation of national accounts, on the other hand, has become a practical necessity and they have to be prepared everywhere at least once a year. The input-output tables can only be integrated with the national accounts in the years for which they are prepared. In these years it would be statistically as well as administratively a great advantage for there to be close collaboration in the preparation of both.

The data on the industrial origin of gross domestic product commonly shown in a supporting table of the national accounts can be provided on a sounder statistical basis if compiled in conjunction with the data for the input-output tables. Inconsistencies, gaps, and discrepancies in the respective data can more easily be detected in this manner.

IV · FINANCIAL FLOWS ACCOUNTS AND INPUT-OUTPUT TABLES

From what has already been said in this study about each of the individual social accounting systems, and about the integration of the national accounts with the financial flows on the one hand, and with the input-output tables on the other hand, it is evident that an integration of financial flows accounts with the input-output tables is conceptually not feasible and is statistically impracticable. The national accounts review committee in its report to the US sub-committee on economic statements emphatically expressed this view in the following words:

Neither in theory nor in practice is there a close relationship between flow of funds statements and input-output tables. Indeed these two aspects of a comprehensive national accounting system are about as far removed conceptually and statistically as is possible within that system. The flow of funds statement emphasises financial flows and collects all its data on an enterprise data. Input-output tables omit financial transactions altogether, concentrate on flow of goods and services among producers, and must be derived from very detailed data collected on a plant and preferably even on a process basis [60, p. 238].

Those who advocate the integration of all the social accounting systems do not normally consider a direct linking of the input-output tables with the financial flows. They do, however, implicitly regard the national accounts system as a linking set of accounts between the input-output tables and the financial flows as well as the financial assets and liabilities. This study has attempted to point out the basic differences in orientation between the national accounts system and the flow of funds system. It has also pointed out that some of the financial transactions are connected with government monetary control. Financial data for these and other related purposes are required on a monthly or quarterly basis. In the matter of periodical reporting, financial accounts definitely differ from the input-output tables. It has also been shown that the development of the present structure of the flow of funds must tend towards a distinct financial orientation and towards accounts of stock rather than accounts of flow. In the process it should end by adopting a methodological structure still more independent of the input-output tables. The national accounts system would then not have to act as a gateway of Janus for these two systems with their different orientations.

Bibliography

1. ADY, PETER and COURCIER, MICHEL: *Systems of National Accounts in Africa.* OEEC. Paris, Dec. 1960.
2. ALLAKHVERDIYAN, D.: 'Natsional'ny dokhod USSR' – *Gospolitizdat,* Moscow, 1958.
3. BOUDERVILLE, JACQUES R.: 'Wassily Leontief et l'etude dynamique du circuit economique, *Revue economique,* No. 6, Nov. 1953.
4. BOWLEY, A. L.: *Studies in the National Income 1924–1938,* Cambridge University Press, 1944.
5. BOWLEY, A. L. PROFESSOR and SIR JOSIAH STAMP: 'Three studies on the national income', *Series of reprints of scarce works on political economy* No. 6 – The London School of Economics and Political Science, 1938.
6. CANADA: *The Interindustry flow of goods and services, Canada 1949;* Reference paper No. 72, Dominion Bureau of Statistics, Ottawa 1956.
7. CANADA: *Supplement to the Interindustry flow of goods and services, Canada 1949;* Supplement to Reference paper No. 72, Dominion Bureau of Statistics, Ottawa 1960.
8. CHALMERS, GEORGE: *An estimate of the comparative strength of Great Britain,* London, 1804.
9. CLARK, COLIN: *National income and outlay,* Macmillan & Co., 1938.
10. COPELAND, MORRIS A.: *A study of moneyflows in the United States,* National Bureau of Economic Research, Inc. 1952.
11. DORFMAN, ROBERT: 'The nature and significance of input-output; *The Review of Economics and Statistics,* XXXVI No. 2, May 1954.
12. DORRANCE, GRAEME S.: *International Monetary Fund – A Review of the present status of financial accounting,* DM/60/18 of 31 May, 1960.

13. EVANS, W. D. and HOFFENBERG, M.: 'The interindustry relations study of 1947'; *The Review of Economics and Statistics*, Vol. XXXIV No. 2, May 1952.

14. FOULKE, ROY A.: *Practical financial statement analysis*, McGraw Hill Book Co., 1953, third edition.

15. FRANCE: 'Rapport sur les comptes de la nation, methodes. '*Janvier – Février 1956 – 8 année, 85–86 supplément*. Ministère des Finances; statistique & études Financières, Paris.

16. FRANCE: Les comptes de la nation, *Vol. I, les comptes, Supplément 12e année, 140, Aout*, 1960. Ministère de Finances, Statistique études Financières, Paris.

17. FRANCE: 'Les comptes de la nation', *Vol. II, les methodes, supplément 12e Année, 141, Septembre 1960*, Ministère des finances, statistique & Etudes Financières, Paris.

18. FRANCE: 'Rapport sur les comptes de la nation de l'année, 1960; Ministère des finances: Statistique & études financières, Juillet 1961, Paris.

19. GEARY, R. C.: Introduction. Studies in social and financial accounting: *Income and Wealth* series *IX*, Bowes and Bowes, London, 1961.

20. GILBERT, MILTON and KRAVIS IRVING, B.: *An International comparison of national products and the purchasing power of currencies* – OEEC 1954.

21. HICKS, J. R.: *The Social framework, an introduction to economics*, 3rd edition, Oxford at the Clarendon Press 1960.

22. HOOD, WM. C.: *Financing of economic activity in Canada; including a presentation of National Transaction Accounts for Canada 1945 – 54*, by Read, L. M., Handfield-Jones, S. J. and Emmerson, F. W. Royal Commission on Canada's economic prospects 30 July, 1958.

23. INTERNATIONAL MONETARY FUND: *Balance of Payments Manual;* 3rd edition, July 1961, Washington.

24. KOLGANOV, M. V.: *Natsional'ny dokhod – Ocherki po istorii i teoyii voprsa* – Gospolitizdat, Moscow 1959.

25. KOLGANOV, M. V.: *Metodika perescheta natzionalnogo dokhoda SSHA*, Voprosy ekonomiki, 1955, No. 11.

26. KUZNETS, S.: *National Income and its composition 1919–1938*, National Bureau of Economic Research, New York, 1941.

27. LEONTIEF, WASSILY W.: *The Structure of American economy 1919–1939*, New York, Oxford University Press, 1951, second edition.

28. OEEC: *A standardised system of national accounts*, 1958 edition, Paris, 1959.

29. OEEC: *Statistics of sources and uses of finance 1948–1958*, Paris, 1960.

30. PIGOU, A. C.: *The Economics of Welfare*, Macmillan & Co. Ltd., fourth edition, 1946.

31. POWELSON, JOHN P.: *National Income and Flow of Funds analysis:* McGraw-Hill Book Co. Inc., 1960.

32. READ, L. M.: 'The development of National transactions accounts: Canada's version of or substitute for Money Flows Accounts'; *The Canadian Journal of Economics and Political Science, Vol. XXIII*, Feb. 1957.

33. SCHUMPETER JOSEPH A.: *History of economic analysis* (edited from manuscript by Elizabeth Boody Schumpeter) New York, Oxford University Press 1954.

34. STONE, RICHARD: *Quantity and price indexes in national accounts.* OEEC, Paris.

35. STUVEL, G.: 'A system of national and domestic accounts;' *Economics*, Vol. *XXII*, Aug. 1955.

36. UNITED KINGDOM: *National Income Statistics – Sources and methods*, Central Statistical Office, London, 1956.

37. UNITED KINGDOM: *National Income and Expenditure* 1960, Central Statistical Office, London, 1961.

38. UNITED KINGDOM: *Input-Output Tables for the United Kingdom*, 1954, Board of Trade and Central Statistical Office, London, 1961.

39. UNITED NATIONS: *Measurement of National Income and the construction of social accounts, with appendix on: Definition and measurement of the National Income and related totals* by Richard Stone, Geneva, 1947.

40. UNITED NATIONS: A system of national accounts and supporting tables, studies in methods, *Series F. No. 2, Rev. 1*, New York, 1960.

41. UNITED NATIONS: *Yearbook of National Accounts Statistics*, 1960, New York, 1961.

42. UNITED NATIONS: *A study of the points of correspondence and difference between the United Nations system of national accounts and that employed by the U.S.S.R.* E/CN. 3/R.1, April 1958.

43. UNITED NATIONS: *Observations of the Central Statistical Board of the U.S.S.R.*, on the Draft Study of the points of correspondence, etc., E/CN, 3/R, 1/Add. 1, April, 1958.

44. UNITED NATIONS: *Input-Output Tables and analysis* (Memorandum by the Secretary General) E /CN, 3 /266, January 1960.

45. UNITED NATIONS: *Integration of financial flows into a system of national accounts.* St /Stat /Conf. 7 /L.6 April 1959.

46. UNITED NATIONS: *Statistical commission and economic commission for Europe, Conference of European Statisticians; Report of session held in Geneva;* Conf. Eur. Stats /W.G. 11 /37, 11th May, 1960.

47. UNITED NATIONS: *Statistical Commission and Economic Commission for Europe; Conference of European Statisticians; Report of session held in Geneva;* Conf. Eur. Stats /WG. 11 /29, 9th March 1959.

48. UNITED NATIONS: *Economic Bulletin for Europe, Vol.* 8, No. 1, Geneva, May 1956.

49. UNITED NATIONS: *A system of price and quantity indexes for national accounts,* E /CN, 3 /L76 of 27th December, 1957.

50. UNITED NATIONS: *Survey of national accounting practices.* (Memorandum by the Secretary General) E /CN. 3 /291 of 12th February, 1962.

51. UNITED NATIONS AND INTERNATIONAL MONETARY FUND: 'Joint statement on integrated income and financial accounts;' prepared by the International Monetary Fund at the request of the Expert Group on Statistics of changes in financial assets and liabilities of the Conference of European Statisticians.

52. UNITED STATES: *National Income 1951 Edition;* a supplement to the Survey of Current Business, US Dept., of Commerce, Office of Business Economics, Washington, 1951.

53. UNITED STATES: *National Income 1954 Edition;* a supplement to the Survey of Current Business, US Dept. of Commerce, Office of Business Economics, Washington 1954.

54. UNITED STATES: *Income and Output;* a supplement to the Survey of Current Business; US Dept. of Commerce, Office of Business Economics, Washington, 1958.

55. UNITED STATES: *Income and Output;* a supplement to the Survey of Current Business; US Dept. of Commerce, Office of Business Economics, Washington, Aug. 1961.

56. UNITED STATES: *Flow of Funds in the United States,* 1939–1953; Federal Reserve system, Washington, Dec. 1955.

57. UNITED STATES: *Federal Reserve Bulletin of the Federal Reserve System,* Washington, Aug. 1959.

58. UNITED STATES: *Federal Reserve Bulletin of the Federal Reserve System,* Washington, Aug. 1960.

59. UNITED STATES: *Federal Reserve Bulletin of the Federal Reserve System*, Washington, Aug. 1961.
60. UNITED STATES: *Hearings before the Sub-committee on Economic Statistics of the Joint Economic Committee*, Congress of the United States, Washington 1957.
61. USSR: *Narodnoe Khozyaistvo SSSR v 1959 godu Statistitsheski Yejegodnik*, Gostatisdat ZSUSSR, Moscow 1960.
62. YOUNG, RALPH A.: 'Federal Reserve Flow of Funds Accounts'; *International Monetary Fund Staff Papers, Vol. V, No. 3*, Feb. 1957.
63. ZIRLIN, L. M. and PETROV, A. I.: *Burjuaznayia Statistika skrivaet pravdu*, Gospolitizdat, 1953.

Index